Divine Love Came Down

Wisdom from
St. Alphonsus Liguori

Nancy Sabbag, Editor

The Word Among Us Press
9639 Doctor Perry Road
Ijamsville, Maryland 21754
ISBN: 1-59325-000-2
www.wordamongus.org

Wisdom Series Editor: Patricia Mitchell
Cover design: Christopher Ranck

Unless otherwise noted, Scripture quotations are from the Revised
Standard Version of the Bible: Catholic Edition, © 1965 and 1966, by the
Division of Christian Education of the National Council of Churches of
Christ in the U.S.A. All rights reserved. Used by permission. Scripture
quotations noted "Douay" are from the Douay-Rheims Bible.

Made and printed in the United States of America

Library of Congress Cataloging-in-Publication Data
Liguori, Alfonso Maria de', Saint, 1696-1787.
    [Selections. English. 2003]
    Divine love came down! : wisdom from St. Alphonsus Liguori / Nancy
Sabbag, editor.
        p. cm.
    Includes bibliographical references.
    ISBN 1-59325-000-2
    1. Spiritual life—Catholic Church. I. Sabbag, Nancy. II. Title.
BX2350.3.L54213 2003
    248.4'82—dc21
2003042292

Table of Contents

Introduction

Have you ever taken an extended trip across the country or to another part of the world? You probably met new people. Maybe you encountered one person who touched you with a special kindness or gave you some good advice. Even though you lived in two different worlds, as you spent time together, you realized you weren't so very different from each other. You somehow connected and became friends. When you look back on the experience, you're grateful for it.

So it can be with St. Alphonsus Liguori. If you're picking up his works for the first time, you may feel as if you're stepping into foreign territory where you're not sure you belong. After all, his world seems so distant. How could the writings of a Doctor of the Church who lived three hundred years ago still hold any relevance for your life today?

But as you settle down with him, you will quickly discover an inspirational advisor and fellow "spiritual traveler" along life's way. Alphonsus himself wrote all those centuries ago in his *Visits to the Blessed Sacrament and Blessed Virgin:* "It is sweet to everyone to be in the company of a dear friend."

Although Alphonsus' life is a celebrated one, like many of us he also faced challenges, disappointments, and uncertainty. As a young man he struggled to follow his own dreams, but faced violent opposition from a father who tried to steer him into a prestigious career. As a student, he studied hard to excel on his law exams, only to make a careless mistake in a court room years later, marring a stellar reputation. He was nearly arrested in the streets of Naples. Later, as a priest and confessor, he spent many years dealing with difficult people in politically trying situations. He submitted to authority even when he did not agree. And after sacrificing everything to establish the Redemptorist congregation, his most trusted friends betrayed him, leading the pope to dismiss him from his own spiritual community.

Fortunately for us today, Alphonsus' struggles were no match for his strength of will. With a fervor for evangelizing that could not be quenched, Alphonsus wrote more than one hundred books during his nine decades of life. This little volume, *Divine Love Came Down! Wisdom from St. Alphonsus Liguori,* contains excerpts from nine of his major works. It provides a unique look into this saint's indomitable spirit, his brilliant power of reasoning, his passion for moral excellence, and his ability to teach and inspire. Most unmistakable is his unwavering commitment to reach common, everyday people with the truth of the gospel of Jesus Christ.

Alphonsus Maria de Liguori was born in 1696 near Naples, Italy, the eldest son of aristocratic parents. Donna Anna Cavalieri was a woman of deep faith, esteemed in her community. She taught all of her eight children by lesson and example to love God. Don Joseph Liguori was a nobleman who entertained high ambitions for his children and renown for the Liguori name.

It was Don Joseph who chose a career in law for his son. At age twelve, Alphonsus began studying civil and canon law at the Royal University of Naples. For five years, he applied himself to his studies with seriousness and only occasionally took time out to enjoy one of his two favorite recreational activities—playing cards and hunting. But whenever he did, his father rebuked him and urged him to get back to work. Later in life, Alphonsus would joke about his pastime:

"My vision was not quite good enough for hunting; the sport always got the better of me. But, anyway, I have since changed from hunting birds to hunting souls."

Alphonsus finished school when he was sixteen. Passing his bar examinations with high honors, he dedicated himself to gaining more practical knowledge in law for the next two years. During the day he studied under a reputable lawyer, observing sessions of the Naples law courts. During the evening he attended classes in public speaking, read voraciously, and even prepared and tried practice cases.

A Natural Eloquence. When he began his own practice of law in 1715, Alphonsus made a name for himself with his performance in the courtroom. He burned the midnight oil when necessary to prepare a winning case for a client. According to one biographer, "His power of eloquence was so great that he could hold a courtroom spellbound, and he was known to win even opponents over to his side." Within a few years, he was entrusted with some of the most important cases in Naples.

Even amid worldly success, Alphonsus remained strong in his faith and clung to his personal values. He would defend only those causes he considered just, and he won a reputation for being sympathetic and considerate with his clients.

Hoping that a politically advantageous marriage would boost his social standing, Don Joseph tried to handpick a wife for Alphonsus from the young aristocratic ladies in the region. However, after a profound encounter with the Lord during a religious retreat in 1722, Alphonsus made a private vow of celibacy. Soon circumstances would change forever the direction of his life.

In his eight years as a lawyer, Alphonsus never lost any case he accepted—until 1723. In one of the most important cases he ever tried, he failed to uncover one critical document on which the success of the case rested. The opposing attorney took advantage of his error. The public was stunned; his father was mortified. His friends mocked or pitied him. The shame of that moment launched Alphonsus on a months-long, soul-searching journey that led him to minister to the terminally ill at a local hospital. While there, he experienced a revelation in which God told him to leave the secular world and surrender himself to the Lord's purposes. Alphonsus ended his law practice, and gave over to a brother his right of inheritance as the eldest son.

Evangelistic Zeal. Alphonsus had always wanted to be a priest and minister to the poor and the neglected. He applied himself to the study of theology as diligently as he had once studied law. Within a year's time, he had joined the Congregation of the Apostolic Missions as a novice. He preached missions in and around Naples, and was so successful teaching and bringing people to repentance that he began to draw a faithful following.

Three years after quitting his practice of law, he was ordained a priest. The man who was able to influence crowds in the courtroom was equally effective as a preacher. In the early days of his ministry, he would preach to the poor and homeless in the streets and public squares. In clear, simple, and inspiring words, he instructed people in all walks of life about the great love of God. He was also a gentle confessor, believing that "only kindness could win a soul to repentance, snatch it from the devil, and bring it to the arms of Jesus Christ."

Street crowds that followed Alphonsus grew so large that, on one occasion, the police threatened his group with arrest. Alphonsus then formed what became known as the Association of the Chapels. Instead of meeting in the streets, his followers would break into smaller groups and meet during the week in private homes or businesses for teaching, prayer, and instruction. (One hundred years after the Association of the Chapels was founded, there were still one hundred chapels in Naples alone, each numbering more than three hundred members.)

Alphonsus was in constant demand to conduct retreats for sisters in convents. In time, he was instrumental in founding a new order of sisters at Scala, Italy—the Redemptoristine nuns.

Alphonsus' popularity with the churches in Naples remained strong, but this did not deter him from his primary ambition: to minister to the poor and abandoned in rural areas, where there were few priests. Within a year of his return from working with the sisters at Scala, he was encouraged by his spiritual director, Thomas Falcoia, bishop of Castellamare, to follow his inspiration of establishing a new congregation of men to minister to spiritually neglected people in rural areas. Alphonsus decided to go ahead with the plan, but many of his friends spoke against it, accusing him of being fanatical and foolish. Others who sympathized with his objective in private refused to defend his cause in public.

Among those who encouraged him as he began his new work in Scala was a Redemptoristine nun named Sr. Mary Columba. She told him, "Do not fear, for [the Lord] has made you his thief, to rob a large number of souls from the enemy."

A New Congregation. Despite the skepticism, Alphonsus was able to attract four priests and three laymen to join him in Scala for the work of preaching to the poor. The people of Scala were thrilled with Alphonsus' arrival. The religious men inhabited a small residence and lived austerely, depending solely on the meager resources they themselves brought. Alphonsus' intent was for their lives to reflect the purity and piety of their precious Redeemer, from whom they took their name: Congregation of the Most Holy Redeemer.

But all hopes for their mission were short-lived. Major disputes broke out among the men over issues involving the community's rule—so much so that by the following spring, all abandoned Alphonsus except

Vitus Curtius, a lay brother. Alphonsus was heart-sick. His first attempt had failed. He wandered among the hills and cliffs of Scala for days, praying and fasting, wondering why, if God had called him to this work, it should fail.

It was during his time in the hills that the Blessed Virgin appeared to Alphonsus to console him. This gave him a renewed strength, and he was determined not to be discouraged. Later in his life Alphonsus would write volumes of works devoted to the virtues of the Blessed Mother.

Alphonsus made another start at establishing his congregation. He returned to Naples to solicit new members and, amid rejection and skepticism, managed to recruit two priests. The bishop of another neighboring diocese wanted Alphonsus to establish the community in a new location—in an old hermitage in the village of Villa degli Schiavi, about twenty-five miles north of Naples. In 1733, the new institute ministered to five hundred villagers and those in the surrounding regions.

Alphonsus lived a life of extreme poverty and underwent many physical hardships in an effort to remain humble before God. At night he slept on a simple straw mat, or sometimes a plank, and then only for a few short hours. When traveling, he rode a donkey rather than a horse. Routinely he fasted on bread and water.

God's Arrow of Love. During the next several years, the work of the congregation prospered. In 1735, Villa degli Schiavi became the home of the first novitiate of the Redemptorist fathers. Alphonsus wholeheartedly worked with his novices, encouraging them to develop an interior life, to have the right motives for their actions, and to love sacrificially. Between 1735 and 1747, four new houses were established in various locations of the Neapolitan region.

The Redemptorist rule had at its heart the imitation of the life and virtues of Jesus Christ. It also stressed virtues important in the life of Alphonsus: love of God and neighbor, poverty, obedience, and perseverance. The main work of the order was the preaching of missions to the most abandoned people living in rural areas. No hamlet or town, whatever its size, was to be passed over by the missionaries, who were to stay in each place until the spiritual needs of all were satisfied. The Redemptorist monasteries were to be large enough to accommodate those on retreats. Alphonsus himself embarked on many missionary tours, traveling for weeks at a time, tirelessly meeting the needs of the poor. God blessed his preaching with many conversions.

It was during this time that he began writing his masterpiece, *Moral Theology*. Nine editions appeared in his lifetime alone. The strict "rigorist" position was still prevalent in the eighteenth century—a view of God as a taskmaster who held his people to a long list of rules and regulations. For many, Alphonsus' writings were a breath of fresh air. He preached about God's awesome love and abundant mercy. He continually stressed the necessity of seeking God's grace in prayer to fight temptations to sin.

At the beatification of the saint decades later, Pope Pius VII said: "Alphonsus was in God's hands a sharp arrow, which, discharged against vice, strikes now in one place, now in another, in order to promote the honor of God and the salvation of souls. As a sharp arrow, heated by the fire of love, he had wounded the heart of not a few priests, and so inflamed them that they also left all things and followed their Redeemer."

In 1749, after several months of effort to meet the strict requirements of the Vatican in all matters of the foundation and its rule, Pope Benedict XIV gave his approval to the Congregation of the Most Holy Redeemer. However, the king of Naples, Charles III, wielded totalitarian power and resolved not to allow the Church to impinge on his rule. Thus, he had decreed in 1740 "that no one could found a church, monastery, or congregation without the consent of the king." Alphonsus knew the royal court could suppress the growth of the congregation. For this reason, he felt compelled to cultivate the approval of the king.

After a great deal of effort, in 1752 he obtained permission merely to keep the four Neapolitan houses in existence. The king forbade any additional property or any formation of new religious houses, and he still reserved the right to shut down the existing houses at any time. To protect his congregation in the event that the king suppressed the houses in Naples at a future time, Alphonsus established several houses in the Papal States.

When Alphonsus was sixty-six years old and feeling so poorly he was sure he was near the end of his life, Pope Clement XIII appointed him bishop of St. Agatha of the Goths. Alphonsus sent a desperate plea to Pope Clement to relieve him from this duty. But

Pope Clement did not relent. For thirteen years, while suffering from asthma, poor eyesight, and rheumatism that would eventually force his chin into his chest, Alphonsus obediently served as the shepherd of his people. He continued to serve, from a distance, as rector major of his beloved congregation.

The Frosts of Winter. "Persecutions," Alphonsus once said, "are to the works of God what frosts of winter are to plants; far from destroying them, they help them to strike their roots deep in the soil and make them more full of life. What really injures religious orders, and brings the plant to decay like a worm gnawing at the root, are voluntary sins and shortcomings. It is these imperfections we must put an end to. . . . The more violently persecution rages, the more closely must we become attached to Jesus Christ."

In 1767, the frosts of winter began blowing at Alphonsus' door.

A group of officers of the royal court of Naples—two of whom had once been Alphonsus' associates—accused the Redemptorists of violating the 1752 ban on additional property because a fifth house had been opened in the Papal States. Between 1770 and

1774, the royal representatives waged their political and legal battles against Alphonsus. Alphonsus used all his legal skills to plead his case and defend his congregation's right to exist.

At age eighty-five and too frail to fight these legal battles on his own, he trusted a younger priest to represent him in the matter at the royal court. As it turned out, the priest compromised Alphonsus' faith in him. Through a series of betrayals and misunderstandings, Pope Pius VI was led to believe that Alphonsus had consented to a change of rule that the pope had not approved. The pope sent word that the Redemptorists were no longer to obey Alphonsus. In fact, on September 22, 1780, the pope signed a decree dismissing Alphonsus and the members of the Naples houses from the congregation. When Alphonsus heard this tragic news, he broke down and cried.

Alphonsus was in anguish over what had happened to his beloved congregation and sank into a deep depression. However, he faced this trial with the same grace he had shown when faced with disappointments throughout his lifetime. He submitted to God's will and to the authority of the Church. He treated all those who had wronged him with great charity, writing them letters of encouragement to make wise choices for the congregation. He wasn't as much concerned about the wrongful deeds done to him as he was about the people who would go without care if the community were destroyed.

With the strong faith in God that had permeated his life from his youth, he prophesied that after his death, the congregations in the Kingdom of Naples and the Papal States would be reunited and that the community would "spread its wings far and wide." Alphonsus died in 1787 without seeing the reunification. Four years later, his prophecy was fulfilled. Today, the Redemptorists have spread far and wide— preaching the love of Christ to all parts of the world.

A Life of Faith and Service. The fruits of Alphonsus' life of faith and service are abundant. He was a brilliant Church leader who contributed in significant ways to the development of the dogmas on papal infallibility and the Immaculate Conception. He authored well over one hundred pastoral and theological works, some of which have been translated into more than fifty languages. In 1871, after being petitioned by eight hundred bishops and twenty-five heads of religious orders and universities, Pope Pius IX pronounced him a Doctor of the Church.

The sources used for this collection were taken from older English translations of Alphonsus' writings. In order to make these writings more accessible to the modern reader, we have made some minor adaptations to the translation in cases where it would make the English more readable. We pray that Alphonsus' powerful and moving words will draw you closer to your Savior—just as they have for countless readers over the centuries.

In a letter to the priests of the congregation Alphonsus founded, Pope Leo XIII wrote: "Although the writings of the holy Doctor Alphonsus Maria de Liguori have already been spread throughout the world . . . yet it is desirable that they be propagated more and more, and be found in the hands of all. For he very well knew how to adapt Catholic truths to the comprehension of all, to provide for the moral direction of souls, to excite in a wonderful way true piety in the hearts of all, and to show to those who wander in the dark night of the world the road by which they may pass from the power of darkness to the light and to the kingdom of God."

Through his eloquent and passionate writings, Alphonsus is still reaching out to the poor and needy—yes, to us, the modern sojourners in "the dark night of the world." Here is our opportunity—even centuries later—to be in the company of a dear friend.

Let us not pass it up.

Nancy Sabbag
Editor

1

Redeemed!

Of what worth would it be
if the blood of all goats, or even of all men,
were sacrificed to obtain grace for us?
Only the blood of this Man-God, Jesus,
wins for us pardon and eternal salvation

The Incarnation, Birth and Infancy of Jesus Christ

BEFORE THE MESSIAH CAME

Before the coming of the Messiah, who on the earth loved God? He was hardly known in any corner of the world—that is, except in Judea. Even there, how very few loved him when he came! As for the rest of the world, some worshipped the sun, some the animals, some the very stones, and others even lowly creatures. But after the coming of Jesus Christ, the name of God became known everywhere and was loved by many. After the Redeemer was born, God was more loved by men and women within a few years than he had been in the lapse of four thousand years before then and since the creation of mankind.

The Incarnation, Birth and Infancy of Jesus Christ

LET THERE BE FOUND A REDEEMER!

Adam, our first parent, sinned. Ungrateful for the great benefits God had given him, he rebelled by violating God's command not to eat the forbidden fruit. Because of this God was obliged to drive him out of the earthly paradise in this world, and in the world to come to deprive not only Adam, but all his descendants, of the heavenly and everlasting Paradise he had prepared for them after this life. . . .

Then God said, "What delight do I have left in heaven, now that I have lost men, who were my delight?" *My delights were to be with the children of men* (Proverbs 8:31, Douay). Yes, writes St. Thomas, God loves man just as if man were his god, and as if without man he could not be happy. . . . But then the Lord said, "No, I will not lose man. Let there immediately be found a Redeemer who will satisfy my justice on man's behalf and rescue him from the hands of his enemies and from the eternal death." ❧

The Incarnation, Birth and Infancy of Jesus Christ

THE STRUGGLE BETWEEN
MERCY AND JUSTICE

In contemplating our redemption, St. Bernard imagines a struggle between the justice and the mercy of God. Justice says: "I will no longer exist if Adam is not punished; I will perish if Adam does not die." Mercy, on the other hand, says: "If man is not pardoned, I am lost; I will perish if he does not obtain forgiveness." In this debate the Lord decides that, in order to deliver man who was guilty of death, some innocent one must die. . . .

But on earth, no one was innocent. "Therefore," says the Eternal Father, "since there is no one among men who can satisfy my justice, let him who will go to redeem man step forward." The angels, the cherubim, and the seraphim—all are silent; not one replies. One voice alone is heard—that of the Eternal Word, who says, *Here am I! Send me* (Isaiah 6:8).

"Father," says the only-begotten Son, "your infinite majesty which has been injured by man cannot be adequately satisfied by an angel, who is only a creature. And even though you might accept the satisfaction of an angel, consider that, even in spite of the great benefits we have given man, and in spite of so many promises and threats, we have not yet been able to gain man's love because he is not yet aware of the love we have for him. If we want him to love us without fail, what better occasion can we find than if, in order to redeem him, I, your Son, should go to earth and put on human flesh, and by my death pay the penalty he owes. In this manner your justice is fully satisfied and, at the same time, man is thoroughly convinced of our love!"

"But think," answered the Heavenly Father, "think, O my Son, that in taking the burden of man's debt upon yourself, you will have to lead a life full of sufferings!"

"No matter," replied the Son: *Here am I! Send me.*"

"Think that you will have to be born in a cave, the shelter of the beasts of the field. Then you must flee into Egypt while you are still an infant to escape the hands of those men who, even from your tender infancy, will try to take away your life."

"It matters not: *Here am I! Send me.*"

"Think about how, on your return to Palestine, you will lead a most difficult life, passing your days as a simple boy in a carpenter's shop."

"It matters not: *Here am I! Send me.*"

"Think about how when you go forth to preach and to make yourself known, you will have only a few—very few—who will follow you. Most will despise you and call you an impostor, a magician, a fool, a Samaritan. And finally, they will persecute you to such a degree that they will make you die shamefully on a cross through many torments."

"No matter: *Here am I! Send me.*"

The decree was then passed that the Divine Son would be made man, and by doing this, become the Redeemer of men. The Archangel Gabriel speeds on his way to Mary. Mary accepts him for her son: *And the Word became flesh* (John 1:14). So now, behold Jesus in the womb of Mary, having made his entry into the world in all humility and obedience. He says: "Since, O my Father, men cannot make atonement for their offenses by their works and sacrifices, behold me, your Son, now clothed in human flesh, ready to give myself in their place to satisfy your justice with my sufferings and with my death!" *Consequently, when Christ came into the world, he said, "Sacrifices and offerings thou hast not desired, but a body hast thou prepared for me; . . . Then I said, 'Lo, I have come to do thy will, O God,' as it is written of me. . . "* (Hebrews 10:5,7).

So was it for us that, in order to captivate our love, God decided to become man? Yes, it is a matter of faith. As the Holy Church teaches us: "For us men, and for our salvation, he came down from heaven . . . and was made man." Yes, indeed, God has done all of this in order to be loved by us. ∽

The Incarnation, Birth and Infancy of Jesus Christ

HIS LOVE ALONE

He *entered once for all into the Holy Place, taking not the blood of goats and calves but his own blood, thus securing an eternal redemption* (Hebrews 9:12). Of what worth would it be if the blood of all goats, or even of all men, were sacrificed to obtain grace for us? Only the blood of this Man-God, Jesus, wins for us pardon and eternal salvation. But if God himself had not devised this way to redeem us—by dying to save us—whoever would have been able to think of it? His love alone designed it and carried it out. Therefore Job was right when he cried out to this God who loves us so much: What is man, O Lord, that you exalt him? Why is your heart so intent upon loving him? *What is a man, that thou shouldst magnify him, or why dost thou set thy heart upon him?* (Job 7:17, Douay). ✑

The Incarnation, Birth and Infancy of Jesus Christ

THE GREATNESS OF HIS GOODNESS

After conquering Darius and Persia, Alexander the Great wanted to win the affections of the people he captured, so he went about dressed in the Persian costume. The same way, in order to draw the affections of men to himself, our God clothed himself completely as a human, and was made man: *being born in the likeness of men* (Philippians 2:7). By doing this he wished to make known the depth of the love he has for man: *The grace of God has appeared for the salvation of all men* (Titus 2:11).

Man does not love me, God seemed to say, because he does not see me. I want to make myself seen by him and converse with him, and so make myself loved: *Afterward he appeared upon earth and lived among men* (Baruch 3:37).

God's love for man was extreme, and it had been from all eternity: *I have loved you with an everlasting love; therefore I have continued my faithfulness to you* (Jeremiah 31:3). But until this time, it was not understood how great and inconceivable his love was. Then it truly appeared, when the Son of God became a little one in a stable on a bundle of straw: *The goodness and loving kindness of God our Savior appeared* (Titus 3:4). The Greek text reads: *The singular love of God towards men appeared.* St. Bernard says that from the beginning, the world had seen the power of God in the creation, and his wisdom in the government of the world. But only afterward, in the Incarnation of the Word, was it seen "how great was his mercy." Before God became man on earth, men could not conceive of his goodness. Therefore, he took on human flesh, so that, appearing as man, he might make plain to men the greatness of his goodness. ❧

The Incarnation, Birth and Infancy of Jesus Christ

CHRIST GIVES HIMSELF TO US

The birth of Jesus Christ caused joy to the whole world. He was the Redeemer who had been desired for so many years. Therefore he was called the Desire of the Nations and the Desire of the Eternal Hills. Consider that today also the angel announces to us the same great joy he announced to the shepherds: *Behold, I bring you good news of a great joy which will come to all the people; for to you is born this day . . . a Savior* (Luke 2:10-11).

How the people of any country rejoice when the first son is born to their king! Likewise, then, we should celebrate even more when we see that the Son of God has been born and has come down from heaven to visit us.

We were lost and, behold, he came to save us. Behold the Lamb of God, who came to sacrifice himself to obtain for us God's favor and to become our deliverer, our life, our light, and even our food in the most Holy Sacrament!

St. Maximus says this is why Christ chose to be laid in the manger with the animals: in order to make himself our food. "In the manger, where the food of animals is placed, he allowed his limbs to be the eternal food of men." Now, every day, he is born in the Sacrament of the Eucharist by means of the priests and the words of consecration. The altar is the crib, and we go there to feed ourselves on his flesh. Someone may have the desire to hold the Holy Infant in his arms, as the aged Simeon once did. But faith teaches us that when we receive Communion, the same Jesus who was in the manger of Bethlehem is not only in our arms, but also in our breasts. He was born for this purpose, to give himself entirely to us: *For to us a child is born, to us a son is given* (Isaiah 9:6).

The Incarnation, Birth and Infancy of Jesus Christ

THE FLOWER OF THE FIELD

Arise, everyone! Mary invites all—rich and poor, the just and sinners—to enter the cave of Bethlehem, to adore and to kiss the feet of her newborn Son. Go in, then, all of you devout men and women. Go in and see the Creator of heaven and earth on a little hay in the form of a little infant, so beautiful that he sheds rays of light all around him. Now that he is born and is lying on the straw, the cave is no longer a horrible place, but is now a paradise. Let us enter and not be afraid.

Jesus is born; he is born for all, for each one who desires him: *I am the flower of the field, and the lily of the valleys* (Canticles 2:1, Douay). He calls himself the Lily of the Valley to show us that, as he was born in such great humility, so it is only the humble who find him. Therefore the angel did not go and announce the birth of Jesus Christ to Caesar or to Herod, but to poor humble shepherds. He also calls himself the Flower of the Field because he shows himself in such a way that all can see him. . . . Flowers in gardens are shut up and enclosed between walls; not everyone is permitted to come and gather them. But the flowers of the field are open to all, and anyone who likes may take them. So does Jesus Christ desire to be accessible to all who desire him. ❧

The Incarnation, Birth and Infancy of Jesus Christ

THIS SWEET PROMISE

*G*reater love has no man than this, that a man lay down his life for his friends (John 15:13). What more could your God do than to give his life in order to make you love him? To give his life is the greatest sign of affection one can give to another person who is his friend. What love our Creator has shown us in choosing to die for us, his creatures! This is what St. John was considering when he wrote: *By this we know love, that he laid down his life for us* (1 John 3:16). Indeed, if faith did not teach us that God has been willing to die to show us his love, who would ever be able to believe it?

Ah, my Jesus, . . . I thank you for your mercy and for promising to forgive those who repent. Trusting then in this sweet promise, I hope for your pardon, repenting with all my heart for having so often turned against your love. Since your love has not abandoned me, I consecrate myself to you. You have finished your life by dying in agony on a cross. How can I repay you? I consecrate my life to you. . . . Ah, my Redeemer, do not permit me to separate myself from you ever again. Make me always live and die in your embrace. My Jesus, I repeat, make me always live and die united with you.

The Incarnation, Birth and Infancy of Jesus Christ

CHRIST, OUR HOPE

Since the Eternal Father has given us his own Son to be our mediator and advocate with him—and the satisfaction for our sins—we cannot lose hope that we will obtain from God whatever favor we ask of him, if we avail ourselves of the help of such a Redeemer. *Will he not also give us all things with him?* (Romans 8:32). What can God deny us when he has not denied us his Son?

None of our prayers deserves to be heard or granted by the Lord because we do not deserve graces but punishment for our sins. But Jesus Christ, who intercedes for us and offers in our behalf all the sufferings of his life, his blood, and his death, does deserve to be heard. The Father cannot refuse anything to so dear a Son, who offers his price of infinite value. He is innocent. All that he pays to divine justice is to satisfy our debts, and the satisfaction he offers is infinitely greater than all the sins of mankind. It would not be a just thing if a sinner perished after he repented of his sins and offered to God the merits of Jesus Christ, who has already so abundantly atoned for him.

Let us therefore thank God, and hope all things based on the merits of Jesus Christ. ❧

The Incarnation, Birth and Infancy of Jesus Christ

2

His Saving Love

My beloved Redeemer,
you chose to sacrifice yourself in order to obtain
the pardon of my sins.
And how can I return my gratitude to you?
You have done more than enough
to deserve my love.

The Passion and the Death of Jesus Christ

Love Pays Our Penalty

There once was a king, the lord of many kingdoms, who had only one son. The son was so beautiful, holy, and kind that he was the delight of his father, who loved him as much as himself. This young prince had such a great affection for one of his slaves that when he saw that the slave had committed a crime for which he was condemned to death, the prince offered to die in place of the slave. The father, determined to exact justice, was satisfied to condemn his beloved son to death so that the slave might remain free from the punishment he deserved. Thus the son died a criminal's death, and the slave was freed from punishment.

This fact, the like of which has never happened again in this world—and never will happen—is related in the Gospels. There we read that the Son of God, the Lord of the Universe, seeing that man was condemned to eternal death for the punishment of his sins, chose to take upon himself human flesh and by his death pay the penalty due to man: *He was offered because it was his own will* (Isaiah 53:7, Douay). And his Eternal Father caused him to die on the cross to save us: *He . . . did not spare his own Son but gave him up for us all* (Romans 8:32). What do you think of this love of the Son and of the Father?

My beloved Redeemer, you chose to sacrifice yourself in order to obtain the pardon of my sins. And how can I return my gratitude to you? You have done more than enough to deserve my love. I would be most ungrateful if I did not love you with my whole heart. You have given your divine life for me. Now I give you my own life. Yes, I will spend at least what remains of my life in loving you, obeying you, and pleasing you. ❧

The Passion and the Death of Jesus Christ

He Comes as Our Physician

Physicians, if they love their patients, use all their efforts to cure them. But what physician, in an effort to cure the sick man, ever took the disease upon himself? Jesus Christ has been that physician, one who charged himself with our infirmities in order to cure them. He would not be content to send another in his place, but he chose to come himself on this mission of love in order to gain for himself all our love: *Surely he has borne our griefs and carried our sorrows* (Isaiah 53:4). He chose to heal our wounds with his own blood, and by his death deliver us from the eternal death we deserved. In short, he chose to drink the bitter cup of a life of continual sufferings and a painful death to obtain for us life and deliver us from our many evils.

Jesus said to St. Peter, *Shall I not drink the cup which the Father has given me?* (John 18:11). It was necessary, then, that Jesus Christ suffered so many humiliations to heal our pride; that he embraced a life of such poverty to cure our covetousness; that he was overwhelmed in a sea of troubles, and even died of pure sorrow, to cure our eagerness for earthly pleasures.

The Incarnation, Birth and Infancy of Jesus Christ

He Comes as a Child

Little children readily give anything that is asked of them. Jesus came into the world as a child in order to show that he was ready and willing to give us all good gifts: *in whom are hid all the treasures* (Colossians 2:3). *The Father . . . has given all things into his hand* (John 3:35). If we wish for light, he has come on purpose to enlighten us. If we wish for strength to resist our enemies, he has come to give us comfort. If we wish for pardon and salvation, he has come to pardon and save us. If, in short, we desire the sovereign gift of his love, he has come to inflame our hearts with it. Above all, he has chosen to come as a child to show himself worthy of our love; he comes poor and humble to take away our fear and to win our affections.

Jesus has chosen to come as a little child to make us love him not only with an appreciative love, but even a tender love. All infants attract the tender affection of those who see them. Who does not love a God, with all the tenderness they have, whom they see as a little child, in need of milk to nourish him, trembling with cold, poor, lowly and forsaken, weeping and crying in a manger, and lying on straw? It was this that caused the loving St. Francis to exclaim: "Let us love the child of Bethlehem, let us love the child of Bethlehem." Come, love a God who has come as a child, poor and so sweet, and has come down from heaven to give himself entirely to you. 〜

The Incarnation, Birth and Infancy of Jesus Christ

SO HIGH A COST

Jesus Christ could have easily obtained salvation for us without suffering and by leading a life of ease and delight. But no, *for the joy that was set before him [he] endured the cross* (Hebrews 12:2). He refused the riches, the delights, and the honors of the world, and chose for himself a life of poverty and a death full of suffering and disgrace. And why? Wouldn't it have been enough for him to offer to his Eternal Father one single prayer for the pardon of man? Such a prayer, being of infinite value, would have been not only sufficient to save the world, but infinite worlds besides. Why, then, did he choose for himself so much suffering and a death so cruel? Why so high a cost in order to save man?

St. John Chrysostom answers that a single prayer of Jesus would indeed have been sufficient to redeem us, but it was not sufficient to show us the love our God has for us: "That which sufficed to redeem us was not sufficient for love.". . . Because Jesus loved us so much, he desired very much to be loved by us. Therefore, he did every-

thing he could—even suffering for us—in order to win
our love and to show there was nothing more he could
do to make us love him: "He endured much weariness,"
says St. Bernard, "that he might bind man to love him
much." ❧

The Passion and the Death of Jesus Christ

SALVATION FOR ALL

The thought that most inflamed St. Paul with the
love of Jesus was that he chose to die, not only for all
men, but for him in particular: *who loved me and gave himself for me* (Galatians 2:20). Yes, he has loved me, Paul
said, and gave himself up to die for my sake. And every
one of us can say the same thing. For St. John
Chrysostom makes it clear that God loves every indi-
vidual man with the same love with which he has
loved the world, and each one of us is under as great an
obligation to Jesus Christ for having suffered for everyone as if he had suffered for us alone. . . .

If he had died for you alone, what great sorrow it
would cause you to think your neighbors, parents,
brothers, and friends would be separated from you forever! If you and your family had been slaves and someone came to rescue you alone, would you not beg him

to save your parents and brothers too? And how much would you thank him if he did this to please you!

Say, therefore, to Jesus: "O my sweetest Redeemer! You have done this for me without my having asked you. You have not only saved me from death at the price of your blood, but also my parents and friends, so that I may have the hope that we will all enjoy your presence for-ever in Paradise together. O Lord! I thank you and I love you, and I hope to thank you for it and to love you for-ever in that blessed country." ❧

The Passion and the Death of Jesus Christ

THE SECRETS OF CHRIST'S HEART

It is a pleasing thing to see a person beloved by some great man, and even more so if the great man has the power to give that person a great fortune. But how much more sweet and pleasing is it to see ourselves beloved by God, who can give us an eternity of happiness? Under the old law, men might have doubted whether God loved them with a tender love. But after having seen him shed his blood on the cross and die for us, how can we doubt that he loves us with an infinite tenderness and affection?

O my soul, look at Jesus hanging from the cross all covered with wounds! See how by these wounds he proves to us the love that is in his enamored heart: "The secrets of his heart are revealed through the wounds of his body," says St. Bernard. ❧

The Passion and the Death of Jesus Christ

LOOKING TO THE LIGHT

T he love of our God has appeared to all men. Why is it, then, that all men haven't known it, and even in our day so many are ignorant of it? This is the reason: *The light has come into the world, and men loved darkness rather than light* (John 3:19). They do not know him because they do not wish to know him, preferring to love the darkness of sin rather than the light of grace.

But let us not be one of these unhappy people. If, in the past, we have shut our eyes to the light, thinking little of the love of Jesus Christ, let us try, during the days that remain to us in this life, to have ever before our eyes the sufferings and death of our Redeemer. Let us love him who has loved us so much, looking for the blessed hope and coming of the glory of the great God and our Savior, Jesus Christ. ❧

The Incarnation, Birth and Infancy of Jesus Christ

A Sign on Our Hearts

An earthly king would be cautious not to humble himself by asking one of his subjects for his love. But God, who is infinite goodness, the Lord of all, almighty and all wise, who deserves an infinite love and who has given us spiritual and temporal gifts, does not hesitate to ask us to love him. He exhorts us and commands us to love him, and still he cannot obtain it. *What does he ask of each one of us but to be loved? What does the* LORD *your God require of you, but to fear the* LORD *your God . . . to love him* (Deuteronomy 10:12). It is as though God, who possesses in himself infinite happiness, could not be happy without seeing himself loved by us: "As if," says St. Thomas, "he could not be happy without you."

We cannot doubt, then, that God loves us exceedingly. Because he loves us so much, he wants us to love him with our whole heart: *Thou shalt love the Lord thy God with thy whole heart* (Deuteronomy 6:5, Douay). And then he adds: *And these words shall be in thy heart, and walking on thy journey, sleeping and rising: and thou shalt bind them as a sign on thy hand, and they shall be and shall move between thy eyes. And thou shalt write them in the entry, and on the doors of thy house* (6:6-9, Douay).

We can see in all these words how earnest is God's desire to be beloved by each one of us. He wants this command of loving him with our whole heart to be imprinted on our hearts. May we never be unmindful of these words. He wishes us to meditate upon them when we are sitting at home and when we are awake. He wishes us to hold them in our hands and bind them up with some significant memento so that wherever we may be, our eyes may always rest upon them. ❧

The Way of Salvation and of Perfection

GOD HAS NOT CEASED TO CALL YOU

Consider the mercy of God when he calls a sinner to repentance. When Adam rebelled against the Lord and hid himself from his face, God goes in search of him and calls to Adam with tears: *Where are you?* (Genesis 3:9).

God has often done the same to you. You fled from God and he sought after you, calling you at one time by his inspiration, at another time by a remorseful conscience, once by sermons, again by trials, and by the death of your friends. Speaking of you, Jesus appears to say: *I have labored with crying; my jaws are become hoarse* (Psalm 68:4, Douay). My son, I have almost lost my voice calling you to repentance. Remember, O sinners, says St. Teresa, that the Lord who will one day be your judge is now calling you to return to him.

Dearly beloved Christian, how often have you been deaf to the calls of God? You don't deserve for him to call you anymore, but your God has not ceased to call you because he wishes to make peace with you and to save you. . . . He places himself at the door of the ungrateful heart: *Behold, I stand at the door and knock* (Revelation 3:20). He even appears to beg us to allow him to enter: *Open to me, my sister* (Song of Solomon 5:2). He grows weary praying for admission: *I am weary of entreating thee* (Jeremiah 15:6, Douay). Yes, says St. Denis, God follows sinners like a despised lover, begging them not to destroy their souls. And this is precisely what the Apostle meant when he wrote to his disciples: *We beseech you on behalf of Christ, be reconciled to God* (2 Corinthians 5:20). The saint means that the sinner does not have to labor to move God to make peace with him, because it is he, and not God, who refuses peace. ❧

Preparation for Death

3

His Willing Sacrifice

Who is there that my
soul should love more tenderly
than a God who has endured scourging
and been drained of his blood for me?
I love you, O God of love!

The Passion and the Death of Jesus Christ

THE HILL OF LOVERS

At whatever period of his life Jesus Christ pre-
sents himself to us, he always appears desirable and worthy of love, whether as an infant in the stable, as a boy
in the shop of St. Joseph, alone meditating in the
desert, or bathed in sweat as he walked about preaching throughout Judea. But in no other form does he
appear more loving than when he is nailed to the cross,
on which he was forced to die because of his immense
love for us. St. Francis de Sales has said that the
Mount of Calvary is the hill of lovers. All love that is
not rooted in the Passion of the Savior is weak.

Let us stop and consider that this man, nailed to the tree of shame, is our true God, and that he is here suffering and dying for nothing but for the love of us. ◠◡

The Incarnation, Birth and Infancy of Jesus Christ

YOUR SIN IS LOVE!

A God taken and bound! What could the angels have said at seeing their king with his hands bound, being led by soldiers through the streets of Jerusalem! And what should we say at the sight of our God, who is content for our sake to be bound as a thief and presented to the judge who will condemn him to death? St. Bernard laments, "What have you to do with chains?" What do criminals and chains have in common with you, O my Jesus, who are infinite goodness and majesty? They belong to us sinners and not to you, who is innocent and the Holy of Holies. St. Bernard goes on to say, "What have you done, my innocent Savior, that you should be condemned this way?" O my dear Savior, you are innocence itself—for what crime have you been condemned? I will tell you, St. Bernard replies: The crime you have committed is that you have too great a love for men. Your sin is love!

My beloved Jesus, I kiss the cords that bind you, for they have freed me from the eternal chains I deserved.

. . . I grieve that I have so grievously insulted you. My God, bind my will to yours with the sweet cords of your holy love, so that I may wish for nothing but what is pleasing to you. May I take your will as the only guide of my life. Just as you have had such great care for my good, may I not care for anything but to love you. ❧

The Incarnation, Birth and Infancy of Jesus Christ

REIGN IN OUR HEARTS

H*ail, King of the Jews!* (Matthew 27:29). Our Redeemer was scornfully saluted by the Roman soldiers. After having treated him as a false king and having crowned him with thorns, they knelt before him and called him king of the Jews, and then, rising up with loud cries and laughter, they struck him and spit in his face. St. Matthew writes: *And plaiting a crown of thorns, they put it on his head . . . And kneeling before him they mocked him, saying, "Hail, King of the Jews!" And they spat upon him, and took the reed and struck him on the head* (Matthew 27:29-30). And St. John adds, *and struck him with their hands* (John 19:3).

O my Jesus! This barbarous crown on your head, this vile reed you hold in your hand, this torn purple garment that covers you with ridicule—these make you known as a king indeed, but a king of love. The crowds say to Pilate, *"We have no king but Caesar"* (John 14:15). My beloved Redeemer, if others will not have you for their king, I accept you and want you to be the only king of my soul. I consecrate my whole self to you—do with me as you please. For this end you have endured contempt, so many sorrows, and death itself, to gain our hearts and to reign there by your love. *For to this end Christ died . . . that he might be Lord both of the dead and of the living* (Romans 14:9). Make yourself, therefore, master of my heart, O my beloved King, and reign and hold sway there forever. You alone will I serve.

The Incarnation, Birth and Infancy of Jesus Christ

HE WAS TRULY MAN

Our most loving Savior, when he had come to the Garden of Gethsemane, began his bitter Passion by—of his own free will—allowing the passions of fear, weariness, and sorrow to come and afflict him with all their torments: *He began to fear and to be heavy* (Mark 14:33, Douay) . . . *to grow sorrowful and to be sad* (Matthew 26:37, Douay).

He began first to feel a great fear of death and of the sufferings he would soon have to endure. But why did he begin to fear? Didn't he willingly offer himself up to endure all these torments? *He was offered because it was his own will* (Isaiah 53:7, Douay). Wasn't he the one who so much desired this hour of his Passion, and who had said shortly before, *I have earnestly desired to eat this passover with you* (Luke 22:15)? Then why is it that he was seized with such a fear of death that he even prayed to his Father to deliver him from it? *My Father, if it be possible, let this cup pass from me* (Matthew 26:39).

St. Bede the Venerable answers this and says, "He prays that the chalice may pass from him, in order to show he was truly man." He, our loving Savior, indeed chose to die for us in order to prove the love he has for us. But in order that men might not suppose he had assumed a supernatural body (as some have blasphemously asserted), or that by virtue of his divinity he died without suffering any pain, he made this prayer to his heavenly Father. He did so not only with a view of being heard, but to make us understand that he died as man and was afflicted with a great fear of death and of the sufferings that would accompany his death.

O most sweet Jesus! You took upon yourself our fearfulness in order to give us your courage in suffering the trials of this life. Be forever blessed for your great mercy and love! O, may all our hearts love you as much as you desire and as much as you deserve! ❧

The Passion and the Death of Jesus Christ

SILENCE BEFORE HEROD

It greatly pleased Herod to see Jesus Christ brought before him. Herod hoped that in his presence, in order to deliver himself from death, Jesus would work one of those miracles he had heard about. Therefore he asked him many questions. But because he did not wish to be delivered from death and because Herod was not worthy of his answers, Jesus was silent and he did not answer him. Then the proud king, along with his court, offered Jesus many insults.

Covering him with a white robe as if declaring him to be an ignorant and stupid fellow, he sent him back to Pilate: *And Herod with his soldiers treated him with contempt and mocked him; then, arraying him in gorgeous apparel, he sent him back to Pilate* (Luke 23:11). St. Bonaventure said: "Herod despised him as if impotent because he worked no miracle; as if ignorant because he answered him not a word; as if idiotic because he did not defend himself."

O Eternal Wisdom, O Divine Word! This is one more suffering you had to bear—that you were treated as a fool, as though you had no sense. So greatly does our salvation weigh on you that for love of us you were not only willing to be reviled, but to be filled with humiliations, just as had already been prophesied: *Let him give his cheek to the smiter, and be filled with insults* (Lamentations 3:30). And how could you bear such love for men, from whom you had received nothing but ingratitude and slights?

Ah, my Jesus, don't chastise me as you did Herod by depriving me of your voice. Herod did not recognize you for what you are; I confess you to be my God. Herod did not love you; I love you more than myself. Do not deny me the voice of your inspiration, even though I have deserved it. Tell me what you want of me, for by your grace I am ready to do all that you will. ∾

The Passion and the Death of Jesus Christ

SO PAINFUL A WALK

Imagine that you meet Jesus as he passes along in this sorrowful journey. As a lamb taken along to the slaughterhouse, so is the loving Redeemer conducted to his death: *like a lamb that is led to the slaughter* (Isaiah 53:7). He is so drained of blood and wearied from his torments that, out of mere weakness, he can barely stand. See him all torn with wounds, with that bundle of thorns upon his head, with that heavy cross upon his shoulders, and with one of those soldiers dragging him along by a rope. Look at him as he goes along, with body bent double, with knees buckling, dripping with blood. So painful is it to walk that at every step he seems ready to die.

Put the question to him: O Divine Lamb, have you not yet had your fill of sufferings? If it is by sufferings that you aim to gain my love, let your sufferings end here, for I wish to love you as you want me to. "No," he replies, "I am not yet content: I shall be content when I see myself die for love of you." And where, O my Jesus, are you going now? "I am going," he answers, "to die for you; do not try to stop me. This only do I ask of you and rec-ommend—that, when you see me actually dead upon the cross for you, you will keep in mind the love I have for you. Bear it in mind, and love me." ❧

The Passion and the Death of Jesus Christ

SIGNS OF HIS TENDERNESS

Yes, my sweet Savior, I see you all covered with wounds. I look into your beautiful face but, O my God, it no longer wears its beautiful appearance. It is disfig-ured and blackened with blood and bruises, and shame-ful spittings: *He had no form or comeliness that we should look at him, and no beauty that we should desire him* (Isaiah 53:2). But the more I see you so disfigured, O my Lord, the more beautiful and lovely you appear to me. And what are these disfigurements but signs of the ten-derness of that love you have for me?

I love you, my Jesus, wounded and torn to pieces for me. I wish I could see myself torn to pieces for you, like so many martyrs whose fate this has been! But if I cannot offer you wounds and blood, I offer you at least all the pains it will be my lot to suffer. I offer you my heart, and with this, a desire to love you more tenderly even than I am able. And who is there that my soul should love more tenderly than a God who has endured scourging and been drained of his blood for me? I love you, O God of love! I love you, O infinite Goodness! I love you, O my love, my all! I love you, and I would never cease to say, both in this life and in the other, I love you, I love you, I love you. Amen.

The Passion and the Death of Jesus Christ

HOPE IN THE BLOOD OF CHRIST

H*e was despised and rejected by men; a man of sorrows* (Isaiah 53:3). Now let him who wishes to see this man of sorrows foretold by Isaiah look at Jesus Christ dying on the cross. There, nailed by his hands and feet he hangs, the whole weight of his body pressing on his wounds and his members all torn and bruised. He suffers continual and excruciating pains. Whichever way he turns, his pain increases more and more until it deprives him of life. And thus this man of sorrows is condemned by the Father to die of sheer sufferings on account of our sins.

What Christian, then, O my Jesus, knowing by faith that you have died upon the cross for love of him, can live without loving you? Pardon me then, O Lord, first of all, for this great sin of having lived so many years in the world without loving you. My beloved Savior, the thought of death fills me with dread, as being the moment when I shall give an account to you of all the sins I have committed against you. But that blood I see flowing from your wounds causes me to hope for pardon from you. 〜

The Way of Salvation and of Perfection

I Thirst

Considering these words "I thirst," which Jesus uttered on the cross when he was dying, St. Laurence Justinian says that this thirst was not a thirst which resulted from dryness, but one that arose from the ardor of the love Jesus had for us: "This thirst springs from the fever of his love." By these words our Redeemer intended to declare to us more than the thirst of the body. He wanted to declare the desire he had to suffer for us to show us his love and the immense desire he had to be loved by us: "This thirst proceeds from the fever of his love." And St. Thomas says, "By this 'I thirst' is shown the ardent desire for the salvation of the human race." ❧

The Passion and the Death of Jesus Christ

HE KNEW HIS DESTINY

God, in his compassion for us, does not generally reveal to us the trials that await us before the time we are to endure them. If a criminal who was to be executed on a cross was told at the earliest age of understanding that torture awaited him, could he even be capable of joy? If Saul from the beginning of his reign had known the sword that was to pierce him, if Judas had foreseen the cord that was to suffocate him, how bitter would their lives have been!

But our kind Redeemer, even from the first instant of his life, had always present before him the scourges, the thorns, the cross, the outrages of his Passion, and the desolate death that awaited him. When he beheld the animals that were sacrificed in the temple, he well knew they were figures of the sacrifice that he, the Immaculate Lamb, would one day consummate on the altar of the cross. When he beheld the city of Jerusalem, he well knew he was there to lose his life in a sea of sorrows and reproaches. When he saw his dear mother, he already imagined he saw her in an agony of suffering at the foot of the cross, near his dying self.

Jesus, you accepted and suffered everything for my sake. . . . O my Lord, make me know the greatness of your love in order that I may no longer be ungrateful to you. ❧

The Passion and the Death of Jesus Christ

His Enduring Presence

O that we were
as faithful
with God
as he is with us!

The Holy Eucharist

NEVER ONE HOUR OF SEPARATION

Because he is so great, our God is in every place. There are two places above all where he has his dwelling—one is the highest heaven, where he is present by that glory which he communicates to the blessed; the other is upon earth, within the humble soul who loves him: *I dwell in the high and holy place, and also with him who is of a contrite and humble spirit* (Isaiah 57:15). Our God dwells in the height of heaven and yet he never fails to occupy and engage himself day and night with his faithful servants in their homes. There he gives them his comfort, which surpasses all the delights the world can give. These are deserved by everyone who has ever experienced them: *O taste and see that the LORD is good* (Psalm 34:8).

There are times when friends in the world spend hours conversing together and times when they spend hours apart. But between God and you, if you wish, there shall never be one hour of separation: *When you lie down, your sleep will be sweet* (Proverbs 3:24); *For the Lord will be at thy side* (3:26, Douay). You may sleep, and God will himself be at your side and watch you continually: *I shall find rest with her, for companionship with her has no bitterness, and life with her has no pain, but gladness and joy* (Wisdom 8:16). When you rest, he will not leave your pillow. He remains thinking of you always, so when you wake in the night, he may speak to you by his inspirations and receive from you some act of love, offering, or thanksgiving. Even in those hours, he keeps up his gracious and sweet conversation with you. Sometimes he will speak to you in your sleep and cause you to hear his voice so that when you awake, you may put into practice what he has spoken: *I speak with him in a dream* (Numbers 12:6).

He is also near in the morning, to hear from you some words of affection and confidence, to be the object of your first thoughts and of all the actions you promise to perform that day to please him—and of all the griefs, too, which you offer to endure willingly for his glory and love. But as he never fails to be with you at the moment of your waking, do not fail on your part to give him immediately a look of love and to rejoice when your God announces to you the glad tidings that he is not far from

you—as once he was because of your sins—and that he
loves you, and wants to be loved by you. ❧

The Way of Salvation and of Perfection

YOU HAVE SPENT YOURSELF FOR ME

H*aving loved his own who were in the world, he loved
them to the end* (John 13:1). The love of friends increases
at the time of death, when they are at the point of being
separated from those they love. It is then they try
more than ever, by some pledge of affection, to show the
love they bear toward one another. Similarly, Jesus, during his whole his life, gave us signs of his affection, but
when he came near the hour of his death, he wished to
give us a special proof of his love. What greater proof
could this loving Lord show us than by giving his
blood and his life for each of us? And not content with
this, he left this very same body, sacrificed for us upon
the cross, to be our food, so that the one who receives
it would be wholly united to him, and that love should
mutually increase.

O infinite goodness! O infinite love! Ah, my Jesus,
fill my heart with your love, so I may forget the world and
myself, and think of nothing but of loving and pleasing
you. I consecrate to you my body, my soul, my will, and

my liberty. Up until this time I have looked to gratify myself, to your great displeasure. I am exceedingly sorry for it, my crucified love. From now on I will seek nothing but you, my God and my all.

My God, you are my all. I wish for you alone and nothing more. O that I could spend myself entirely for you, who have spent yourself entirely for me! ❧

The Incarnation, Birth and Infancy of Jesus Christ

THE EUCHARIST:
GREAT PLEDGE OF HIS LOVE

St. Paul remarks on the time Jesus chose to give us the gift of the most Holy Sacrament—a gift that surpasses all the other gifts an Almighty God could give. . . . The Apostle tells us that *the Lord Jesus on the night when he was betrayed took bread, and when he had given thanks, he broke it, and said, This is my body which is for you* (1 Corinthians 11:23-24). It was that same night, when men were thinking of preparing torments and death for Jesus, that our beloved Redeemer thought of leaving for them himself in the Blessed Sacrament, thereby making us understand that his love was so great that, instead of being cooled by so many injuries, it was then more than ever yearning towards us. O most loving Savior, how could you have so great a love for men as to remain with them on this earth to be their food after they had driven you away with so much ingratitude!

Let us also think about the immense desire Jesus had during his life for the arrival of that night when he had determined to leave us this great pledge of his love. For at the moment he instituted this most sweet sacrament, he said, *I have earnestly desired to eat this passover with you* (Luke 22:15). These words reveal to us the ardent desire he had to unite himself to us in Communion through the love he has for us. "This is the voice of most burning charity," says St. Laurence Justinian. And Jesus still retains the same desire toward all those who love him now. There is not a bee, God said one day to St. Matilda, that throws itself with such eagerness upon the flowers in order to suck out the honey as I, through the violence of my love, hasten to the soul that desires me.

The Passion and the Death of Jesus Christ

FOUNTAINS OF GRACE

We have three fountains of grace in Jesus Christ. The first is the fountain of *mercy*, where we may purify ourselves from all the filth of our sins. Our blessed Redeemer formed this fountain for us out of his own blood for our good. *To him who loves us and has freed us from our sins by his blood* (Revelation 1:5).

The second fountain is that of *love*. He who meditates on the sufferings endured by Jesus Christ for the love of us, from his birth even until his death, must feel inflamed with that blessed fire that Christ came to earth to enkindle in the hearts of men. So it is that the waters of this fountain wash and at the same time inflame our souls. . . .

The third fountain is that of *peace*. This is what Jesus Christ meant when he said, *If any one thirst, let him come to me* (John 7:37). He who desires peace of mind, let him come to me, the God of peace. The peace the Lord gives to those who love him is not the peace the world promises in sensual pleasures or in temporal goods, which do not satisfy the heart of man. The peace God gives to his servants is true peace, perfect peace, which satisfies the heart and surpasses all the enjoyments that creatures can afford. *But whoever drinks of the water that I shall give him will never thirst* (4:14). ✍

The Incarnation, Birth and Infancy of Jesus Christ

THE THREAD OF GOD'S GRACE

We all ought to feel we are standing on the edge of a precipice, suspended over the abyss of all sins and supported only by the thread of God's grace. If this thread fails us, we will certainly fall. *If the Lord had not been my help, my soul would soon have dwelt in the land of silence* (Psalm 94:17).

It is a matter of faith that without the aid of grace, we cannot do any good work, nor even think a good thought. "Without grace men do no good whatever, either in thought or in deed," says St. Augustine. As the eye cannot see without light, so says the holy Father, man can do no good without grace.

The Apostle Paul had said the same thing: *Not that we are competent of ourselves to claim anything as coming from us; our competence is from God* (2 Corinthians 3:5). And David said it before St. Paul: *Unless the LORD builds the house, those who build it labor in vain* (Psalm 127:1). In vain does man weary himself trying to become a saint unless God lends a helping hand: *Unless the LORD watches over the city, the watchman stays awake in vain* (127:1). If God did not preserve our souls from sins, in vain would we be trying to preserve our souls by our own strength. Therefore the holy prophet David protested, *not in my bow do I trust* (Psalm 44:6). I will not hope in my arms, David said, but only in God, who alone can save me. ❧

The Great Means of Salvation and of Perfection

In His Presence

St. Teresa said that in this world it is impossible for all the subjects [of a king] to speak directly to the king. As for the poor, the most they can hope for is to speak with him by means of some third person. But to speak with you, O King of Heaven, there is no need for a third person, for everyone who wishes can find you in the Most Holy Sacrament and can speak to you at his pleasure and without restraint. For this reason, said St. Teresa, Jesus Christ has concealed his majesty in the sacrament under the appearance of bread, to give us more confidence and to take away our fear of approaching him.

Oh how Jesus seems continually to exclaim from the altar: *Come to me, all who labor and are heavy laden, and I will give you rest* (Matthew 11:28). Come, he says, come, you poor; come, you infirm; come, you afflicted; come, you just and you sinners, and you will find in me a remedy for all your losses and troubles. So great is Jesus Christ's desire to console everyone, that he remains day and night on our altars so he may be found by all and may grant favors for all. That is why the saints experienced in this world such pleasure remaining in the presence of Jesus in the Blessed Sacrament, the reason days and nights appeared to them as moments. O, if Jesus were our whole love, days and nights in his presence would appear to us as moments, too. ❧

The Holy Eucharist

THE HEAVENLY BREAD

When Jesus comes to a person in Holy Communion, he brings to him every grace and especially the grace of perseverance. This is the principal effect of the Most Holy Sacrament of the Altar—to nourish those who receive this food of life, to give them great strength to become holy, and to resist those enemies who desire our death. That is why Jesus, in this sacrament, calls himself heavenly bread: *I am the living bread which came down from heaven; if any one eats of this bread, he will live for ever* (John 6:51). Even as earthly bread sustains the life of the body, so this heavenly bread sustains the life of the soul by making it persevere in the grace of God.

The Council of Trent teaches that Holy Communion is that remedy which delivers us from daily faults and preserves us from mortal sins. Pope Innocent III writes that by his Passion, Jesus Christ delivers us from sins we have committed, and by the Holy Eucharist he delivers us from sins we might commit. St. Bonaventure says that sinners must not stay away from Communion because they have been sinners. On the contrary, they ought to receive it more frequently for this very reason, because "the more infirm a person feels himself, the more he is in want of a physician." ∾

The Holy Eucharist

THE FAITHFUL HEART OF JESUS

O how faithful is the beautiful heart of Jesus towards those he calls to his love: *He who calls you is faithful, and he will do it* (1 Thessalonians 5:24).

The faithfulness of God gives us confidence to hope all things, although we deserve nothing. If we have driven God from our heart, let us open the door to him and he will immediately enter, according to the promise he has made: *If any one hears my voice and opens the door, I will come in to him and eat with him* (Revelation 3:20). If we wish for graces, let us ask God for them in the name of Jesus Christ, for he has promised us that we shall obtain them: *If you ask anything of the Father, he will give it to you in my name* (John 16:23). If we are tempted, let us trust in him, and he will not permit our enemies to tempt us beyond our strength: *God is faithful, and he will not let you be tempted beyond your strength* (1 Corinthians 10:13).

O how much better it is to have to deal with God than with men! How often do men promise and then fail, either because they tell lies in making their promises or because, after having made the promise, they change their minds: *God is not a man, that he should lie, nor as the son of man, that he should be changed* (Numbers 23:19, Douay). God cannot be unfaithful to his promises because, being truth itself, he cannot lie nor change his mind since all that he wills is just and right. He has promised to receive all who come to him, to give help to him who asks it, to love him who loves him. Wouldn't he do it then? *Hath he said, then, and will he not do it?* (23:19, Douay). Oh that we were as faithful with God as he is with us! ❧

The Holy Eucharist

NOTHING CAN TROUBLE US

The Lord said in Isaiah: *Can a woman forget her sucking child, that she should have no compassion on the son of her womb? Even these may forget, yet I will not forget you. Behold, I have graven you on the palms of my hands* (Isaiah 49:15-16). He has engraved us in his hands with his own blood. Therefore, we shouldn't trouble ourselves about anything, since everything is ordained by those hands that were nailed to the cross as a testament to the love he has for us.

Nothing can trouble us so much that Christ cannot reassure us. Let the sins I have committed surround me, let the devil lay snares for me, let fears for the future threaten me. By demanding mercy of the most tender Jesus Christ, who has loved me even to the point of death, I cannot possibly lose confidence, for I see myself so highly valued that God gave himself for me. O my Jesus, you are a sure haven for those who seek you in time of peril! O most watchful Pastor, a person who does not trust in you deceives himself; it would be better if he would choose to reform his life!

Therefore you have said: "I am here, fear not; I am he who afflicts and who consoles. From time to time, I place some people in desolations that seem equal to hell itself, but after a while I bring them out and console them. I am your advocate who has made your cause my own. I am your surety and have come to pay your debts. I am your Lord who has redeemed you with my blood, not in order to abandon you, but to enrich you, having bought you at a great price. Would I fly from him who seeks me when I went forth to meet those who sought to kill me? I did not turn away my face from him who struck me; shall I turn away from him who would adore me? How can my children doubt that I love them, seeing that out of love for them I placed myself in the hands of my enemies? Who have I ever despised that loved me? Who have I ever abandoned that sought my aid? I even go seeking those who do not seek me." ◌

The Holy Eucharist

5

What Prayer Accomplishes

I do not think I have written
a more useful work than this one,
in which I speak of prayer as a necessary
and certain means of obtaining salvation
and all the graces we require toward that end.

The Great Means of Salvation and of Perfection

THE VALUE OF OUR PRAYERS

Our prayers are so dear to God that he has appointed the angels to present them to him as soon as they come out of our mouths. "The angels," says St. Hilary, "preside over the prayers of the faithful and offer them daily to God." This is that *smoke of the incense . . . with the prayers of the saints* (Revelation 8:4), which St. John saw ascending to God from the hands of the angels, and which he saw in another place represented by golden vials full of sweet odors, very acceptable to God. But in order to better understand the value of our prayers in God's sight, it is helpful to read the numerous promises God makes to the person who prays, as found in both the Old and New Testaments. *Call upon me in the day of trouble; I will deliver you* (Psalm 50:15).

Call to me and I will answer you (Jeremiah 33:3). *Ask, and it will be given you; seek, and you will find; knock, and it will be opened to you* (Matthew 7:7). *How much more will your Father who is in heaven give good things to those who ask him?* (Matthew 7:11). *Every one who asks receives, and he who seeks finds* (Luke 11:10). *Ask whatever you will, and it shall be done for you* (John 15:7). *About anything they ask, it will be done for them by my Father in heaven* (Matthew 18:19). *Therefore I tell you, whatever you ask in prayer, believe that you have received it, and it will be yours* (Mark 11:24). *If you ask anything in my name, I will do it* (John 14:14). *Truly, truly, I say to you, if you ask anything of the Father, he will give it to you* (John 16:23). There are a thousand similar texts, but it would take too long to quote them all.

God wills us to be saved, but for our greater good he wills us to be saved as conquerors. Therefore, while we remain here we have to live in continual warfare and if we want to be saved, we have to fight and conquer. "No one can be crowned without victory," says St. John Chrysostom. We are very feeble, and our enemies are many and mighty. What makes us able to stand against them or defeat them?

St. Laurence Justinian says that by praying, we build for ourselves a strong tower, where we shall be secure from all the snares and assaults of our enemies. . . . Yes, by prayer we obtain God's help, which is stronger than any created power. ❧

The Great Means of Salvation and of Perfection

PRAYER: A SECURE ANCHOR

What is prayer? St. John Chrysostom says it is "the anchor of those tossed on the sea, the treasure of the poor, the cure of diseases, the safeguard of health." It is a secure anchor for those in peril of shipwreck; it is a treasury of immense wealth for those who are poor; it is the most effective medicine for those who are sick; and it is a sure preservative for those who want to keep themselves well. What does prayer accomplish? Let us hear St. Laurence Justinian: "It pleases God, it gets what it asks, it overcomes enemies, it changes men." It appeases the wrath of God, who pardons all who pray with humility. It obtains every grace asked for. It vanquishes all the strength of the tempter, and it changes men from blind into seeing, from weak into strong, from sinners into saints. ❧

The Great Means of Salvation and of Perfection

GO NEAR TO GOD

*L*ighten my eyes, lest I sleep the sleep of death (Psalm 13:3). May he cause the light of his countenance to shine upon us (Psalm 66:2, Douay). Teach me the way I should go (Psalm 143:8). Give me understanding that I may learn thy commandments (Psalm 119:73).

To receive divine light, we must go near to God. *Come ye to him and be enlightened* (Psalm 33:6, Douay). "As we cannot see the sun without the light of the sun itself," says St. Augustine, "so we cannot see the light of God but by the light of God himself." This light is obtained in the spiritual exercises. By them we approach God, and he enlightens us with his light. "Spiritual exercises" means nothing more than that we withdraw ourselves from interaction with the world for a time and go to converse with God alone. There, God speaks to us by his inspirations, and we speak to God in our meditations—by acts of love, by repenting of our sins that have displeased him, by offering ourselves to serve him for the future with all our heart, and by asking him to make his will known to us and to give us strength to accomplish it. . . .

St. Anselm gave the following advice to someone who was worried by many worldly concerns and who complained that he had not a moment of peace: "Leave your concerns and hide yourself for a while from your tumultuous thoughts. Spend a little time contemplating God and rest in him. Say to God, 'Now teach my heart where and how I may seek you, where and how I shall find you.'" These words apply to all of us. Get away for a short time from those earthly occupations that make you restless, he says, and rest quietly with God. Say to him: "O Lord, show me where and how I may find you, that I may speak alone to you, and at the same time hear your words." ❧

The Great Means of Salvation and of Perfection

TRUST IN GOD'S PROMISES

Certainly God would not have exhorted us to ask him for favors if he was not determined to grant them. This is the very thing he exhorts us so strongly to do, and which is repeated so often in the Scriptures—pray, ask, seek, and you shall obtain what you desire: *Ask whatever you will, and it shall be done for you* (John 15:7). And so that we may pray to him with great confidence, our Savior has taught us the Our Father. In this prayer he teaches us that when we are in need of the graces necessary for salvation (all of which are included in the petitions of the Lord's Prayer), we should call him not Lord, but Father—"Our Father." This is because it is God's will that we ask him for grace with the same confidence as a son would who, when in need or when sick, asks his own father for food or medicine. If a son is dying of hunger, he only has to make his case known to his father, and his father will immediately provide him with food. And if he has received a bite from a venomous serpent, he only has to show his father the wound, and the father will immediately apply whatever remedy he has.

Therefore, let us trust in God's promises, always praying with confidence and not vacillating, but being stable and firm. *Let us hold fast the confession of our hope without wavering, for he who promised is faithful* (Hebrews 10:23). As we are perfectly certain that God is faithful in his promises, so through faith we ought to be perfectly certain that he will hear us when we pray. Sometimes, when we are in a state of spiritual dryness or are disturbed by some fault we have committed, we may not feel the sense of confidence while praying that we want to experience. Even so, let us force ourselves to pray, and to pray without ceasing, for God will not neglect to hear us. ∽

The Great Means of Salvation and of Perfection

PRAY WITH CONFIDENCE

The principal instruction St. James gives us, if we wish by prayer to obtain grace from God, is that we pray with a confidence that feels sure of being heard and without hesitating: *Let him ask in faith, with no doubting* (James 1:6). St. Bernard teaches that it is our confidence alone that obtains for us the divine mercies: "Hope alone obtains a place of mercy with you, O Lord."

God is very pleased with our confidence in his mercy because we then honor and exalt his infinite goodness, which he wants us to make known to the world. The royal prophet David says: *Let all them be glad that hope in thee: they shall rejoice for ever, and thou shalt dwell in them* (Psalm 5:12, Douay). God protects and saves all those who confide in him: *He is a shield for all who take refuge in him* (Psalm 18:30). *Thou who savest them that trust in thee* (Psalm 16:7, Douay). Oh the great promises that are recorded in the Scriptures to all those who hope in God! ❧

The Great Means of Salvation and of Perfection

WE ARE WEAK, BUT GOD IS STRONG

God knows how useful it is for us to pray: It keeps us humble and exercises our confidence in him. He therefore permits us to be assaulted by enemies too mighty for us to overcome by our own strength so that by prayer, we may receive from his mercy the aid to resist them. It is especially true that no one can resist the impure temptations of the flesh without submitting himself to God when he is tempted. Our foe, the devil, is so terrible that, when he fights with us, he takes away all light. He makes us forget all our meditations, all our good resolutions; he makes us disregard the truths of faith we have learned, and even almost lose the fear of divine punishments. He conspires with our natural inclinations that drive us with the greatest violence to indulge in sensual pleasures. In such a moment, anyone who does not have recourse to God is lost. The only defense against this temptation is prayer. . . .

It is wrong, then, for sinners to excuse themselves by saying they have no strength to resist temptation. If you don't have the strength, why don't you ask for it? St. James gives this reproof: *You do not have, because you do not ask* (James 4:2). There is no doubt that we are too weak to resist the attacks of our enemies. But, on the other hand, it is certain that God is faithful, as the Apostle says, and will not permit us to be tempted beyond our strength: *God is faithful, and he will not let you be tempted beyond your strength, but with the temptation will also provide the way of escape, that you may be able to endure it* (1 Corinthians 10:13).

We are weak, but God is strong. When we ask him for aid, he communicates his strength to us. We will be able to do all things, as the Apostle Paul reasonably assured himself: *I can do all things in him who strengthens me* (Philippians 4:13). ❧

The Great Means of Salvation and of Perfection

RECEIVE GOD'S FAVOR

Let us mark well the words of St. James: *If any of you lacks wisdom, let him ask God, who gives to all men generously and without reproaching* (James 1:5). All those who pray to God are heard by him without fail and receive grace in abundance: *who gives to all men generously.* You should particularly notice the words that follow: *without reproach.* This means that God does not do as men do. When a person who has previously injured another man asks for a favor, he is immediately reminded of his offense. God does not do this to the person who prays. Even though he may be the greatest sinner in the world, God does not remind him of his offense when he is asking for some grace that will aid his eternal salvation. He does not scold him for the offenses he has committed but, just as if the man had never displeased him, he instantly receives him, consoles him, hears him, and enriches him with an abundance of his gifts.

On top of this, in order to encourage us to pray, our Savior says, *Truly, truly, I say to you, if you ask anything of the Father, he will give it you in my name* (John 16:23). It is as though he is saying, "Courage, O sinners; do not despair. Do not let your sins turn you away from having access to my Father and from hoping to be saved by him, if that is what you desire. True, you do not have any reasons to obtain the graces you ask for, for you only deserve to be punished. But do this: Go to my Father in my name, and through my merits ask the favors you want, and I promise and swear to you (Amen, amen, I say to you, which, according to St. Augustine, is a kind of oath) that whatever you ask, my Father will grant."

O God, what greater comfort can a sinner have after his fall than to know for certain that all he asks from God in the name of Jesus Christ will be given to him! ⧽

The Great Means of Salvation and of Perfection

HE WILL SPEAK TO YOU

In a word, if you desire to delight the loving heart of your God, be careful to speak to him as often as you can and with the fullest confidence that he will not refuse to answer and speak with you in return. It's true—he does not make himself heard in any voice that reaches your ears, but he speaks in a voice that your heart can easily perceive when you withdraw from conversation with people in order to spend time conversing with your God alone: *I will lead her into the wilderness, and I will speak to her heart* (Hosea 2:14, Douay). He will then speak to you by such inspirations, such interior lights, such manifestations of his goodness, such sweet touches in your heart, such tokens of forgiveness, such experiences of peace, such hopes of heaven, such rejoicings within you, such sweetness of his grace, such loving and close embraces—in a word, by many voices of love—that he will be well understood by those whom he loves, and who seek for nothing but him alone. ❧

The Way of Salvation and of Perfection

CAST AWAY YOUR CARES

*B*e anxious for nothing, says St. Paul, *but in everything by prayer and supplication, with thanksgiving let your requests be made known to God* (Philippians 4:6). What is the use, says the Apostle, of agitating yourselves with miseries and fears? Drive away all your cares, which are useless except to lessen your confidence and make you lukewarm and careless in walking along the way of salvation. Pray and seek always, and make your prayers sound in God's ears. Thank him for having promised to give you the gifts you desire whenever you ask for them—namely, effective grace, perseverance, salvation, and everything you desire. The Lord has given us our post in the battle against powerful foes, but he is faithful in his promises and will never allow us to be assaulted more violently than we can resist: *God is faithful, and he will not let you be tempted beyond your strength* (1 Corinthians 10:13). He is faithful, since he immediately cares for those who call on him."

The Great Means of Salvation and of Perfection

6

Conversing with God in All Circumstances

The kings of the earth
give audiences only a few times
in the year, but God gives us
continual audience.

The Great Means of Salvation and of Perfection

SPEAKING TO GOD AT ALL TIMES

Never forget God's sweet presence, as most people do. Speak to him as often as you can, for he does not grow weary of this nor look down on it. If you love him, you will not be at a loss for what to say to him. Tell him all that occurs to you about yourself and your affairs, as you would tell it to a dear friend. Do not look at him as a haughty king who will only converse with the great on great matters. He, our God, delights to converse with us and loves for us to communicate to him our smallest and our most daily concerns. He loves you as much and has as much care for you as if he had no one else but you to think about. He is entirely devoted to your interests, as though his chief purpose were to take care of you, to aid you with his almighty power, to take pity on you with his mercy and goodness, to do you good, and to gain by the delicate touches of his kindness your confidence and love. Show him freely, then, all your state of mind, and pray to him to guide you to accomplish perfectly his holy will. And let all your desires and plans be aimed simply at discovering his good pleasure and doing what is agreeable to his divine heart: *Commit your way to the* LORD (Psalm 37:5). *Ask him that your ways may be made straight and that all your paths and plans may prosper* (Tobias 4:19).

Don't ask, "But why do I need to disclose to God all my wants if he already sees and knows them better than I?" True, he knows them, but God acts as if he does not know your needs unless you speak to him about them or ask for his help. Our Savior knew very well that Lazarus was dead, and yet he acted as if he did not know until Mary had told him of it, and then he comforted her by raising her brother to life again (John 11).

Speaking to God in Your Trials. Therefore, when you are experiencing any sickness, temptation, persecution, or other trouble, go at once and ask him for assistance, that his hand may help you. It is enough for you to present the problem to him; to come in and say, *Behold, O LORD, for I am in distress* (Lamentations 1:20). He will not fail to comfort you or at least give you strength to suffer the trial with patience, and it will turn out to be a greater good to you than if he had altogether freed you from it. Tell him about all the thoughts of fear or sadness that torment you and say to him, "My God, in you are all my hopes; I offer to you this trial, and accept your will for me, but take pity on me—either deliver me out from it or give me strength to bear it." And he will truly keep his promise made in the Gospel to all those who are in trouble, to console and comfort them as often as they seek him: *Come to me, all who labor and are heavy laden, and I will give you rest* (Matthew 11:28).

He will not be displeased when in your misery you go to your friends to find some relief, but he wants you chiefly to come to him. Therefore, in all circumstances, after you have gone to others and they have been unable to comfort your heart, go to your Creator and say to him, "*My friends are full of words* (Job 16:21, Douay). They cannot comfort me, and I don't desire to be comforted by them anymore. You are all my hope, all my love. From you only will I receive comfort, and let my comfort be, on this occasion, to do what pleases you. I am ready to endure this grief through my whole life, through all eternity, if this is your good pleasure. Only help me."

Do not fear that he will be offended if you sometimes gently complain and say to him, *Why dost thou stand afar off, O LORD?* (Psalm 10:1). But say, "You know, Lord, I love you and desire nothing but your love; in pity help me, and do not forsake me." And when the despair lasts long and troubles you greatly, unite your voice to that of Jesus in agony and dying on the cross, and ask for his mercy, saying, *My God, my God, why hast thou forsaken me?* (Matthew 27:46). Let the effect of this be to humble you with the thought that no one who has offended God deserves his consolations at all, and let it enliven your confidence, knowing that God does all things, and permits all, for your good: *In everything God works for good with those who love him* (Romans 8:28). Say with great courage, even when you feel most troubled and dejected: *The LORD is my light and my salvation; whom shall I fear?* (Psalm 27:1). *In thee, O LORD, do I seek refuge; let me never be put to shame* (Psalm 31:1). In this way, keep yourself in peace, knowing there never has been anyone who has placed his hopes in God and was lost. *Think of the Lord with uprightness* (Wisdom 1:1). In these words the wise man exhorts us to have more confidence in God's mercy than dread of God's justice, since God is immeasurably more inclined to grant favors than to punish. As St. James says, *Mercy triumphs over judgment* (James 2:13). Then the Apostle Peter tells us that in all our fears, whether about interests for our time on earth or for eternity, we should commit ourselves completely to the goodness of our God, who has the greatest care for our safety: *Cast all your anxieties on him, for he cares about you* (1 Peter 5:7).

Speaking to God in Your Joys. When you receive pleasant news, do not act like those unfaithful, thankless people who go to God in time of trouble, but in time of prosperity forget and forsake him. Be as faithful to him as you would be to a friend who loves you and rejoices in your good: Go at once and tell him of your gladness, and praise him and give him thanks, acknowledging it all as a gift from his hands. Rejoice in that happiness, knowing that it comes to you because it is his good pleasure. Rejoice, therefore, and comfort yourself in him alone: *I will rejoice in the LORD* (Habakkuk 3:18), and *I will sing to the LORD* (Psalm 13:6).

Speaking to God after Your Have Committed a Fault. Another mark of confidence highly pleasing to your most loving God is this: When you have committed any fault, do not be ashamed to go at once to his feet and seek his pardon. Consider that God is so greatly inclined to forgive sinners that he weeps when they are lost, when they depart far from him and live as dead to his grace. Therefore he lovingly calls them, saying, *Why will you die, O house of Israel? So turn, and live* (Ezekiel 18:31-32). He promises to receive the soul who has forsaken him, as soon as she returns to his arms: *Return to me . . . and I will return to you* (Zechariah 1:3). O, if sinners only knew with what tender mercy the Lord stands waiting to forgive them! *Therefore the LORD waits to be gracious to you* (Isaiah 30:18). O, if they only knew the desire he has, not to chastise but to see them converted so that he may embrace them, that he may press them to his heart! He declares: *As I live, says the Lord* GOD, *I have no pleasure in the death of the wicked, but that the wicked turn from his way and live* (Ezekiel 33:11). He even says: *Come now, let us reason together, says the* LORD: *though your sins are like scarlet, they shall be as white as snow* (Isaiah 1:18). In a word, he has declared that when someone repents of having offended him, he forgets all his sins: *None of the transgressions which he has committed shall be remembered against him* (Ezekiel 18:22).

As soon as you fall into any fault, raise your eyes to God, make an act of love, and humbly confessing your fault, hope with confidence for his pardon and say to him, "*Lord, he whom you love is ill* (John 11:3). That heart which you love is sick, is full of sores: *Heal me, for I have sinned against thee* (Psalm 41:4)." Otherwise, while you remain downcast and disturbed at the fault you have committed, your conversation with God will be short; your trust in him will fail; your desire to love him will grow cold; and you will hardly be able to go forward in the way of the Lord. On the other hand, by going immediately to God to ask for his forgiveness and to promise him that you will reform your life, your very faults will serve to advance you further in his love. Between friends who sincerely love each other, it often happens that when one has displeased the other and then humbles himself and asks pardon, their friendship becomes stronger than ever. You should do likewise; see to it that your very faults serve to bind you yet closer in love to your God.

Speaking to God When in Doubt. In any kind of doubt also, either your own or that of others, never stop acting toward your God with a confidence as that of faithful friends, who consult together on every matter. Take counsel with him and beg him to enlighten you that you may decide on what will be most pleasing to him: *Put thou words in my mouth, and strengthen the resolution in my heart* (Judith 9:18, Douay). Lord, tell me what you would have me to do or to answer, and I will do it. *Speak, for thy servant hears* (1 Samuel 3:10).

Speaking to God for Your Neighbor. Use your freedom with God not only to tell him of your own needs, but also the needs of others. How acceptable it will be to your God that sometimes you even forget your own interests to speak to him about the advancement of his glory, or the miseries of others, especially those who groan in affliction—those souls who in purgatory sigh to see him and poor sinners who are living destitute of his grace! For these especially, say to him: "Lord, you who are so kind, and worthy of an infinite love, how do you endure seeing so many in the world, on whom you have granted so many favors, and who still will not know you, will not love you, and even offend and despise you? Ah! My God, object of all love, make yourself known; show how worthy of love you are. 'Hallowed be thy name, thy kingdom come.' May your name be adored and beloved by all; may your love reign in all hearts. Ah, let me not depart without granting me some grace for those unfaithful people for whom I pray." ❧

The Way of Salvation and of Perfection

1

Responding to God's Love

Does God love you?
Love him.
His delight is to be with you:
Let your delight be to be with him.

The Way of Salvation and of Perfection

HAVE CONFIDENCE IN GOD

Job was struck with wonder when he considered how devoted our God is to benefiting man and that the primary care of God's heart is to love man and to make himself beloved by him. Speaking to the Lord, he exclaims, *What is man, that thou dost make so much of him, and that thou dost set thy mind upon him?* (Job 7:17). It is clearly a mistake to think that showing great confidence and familiarity with God is a lack of reverence to his Infinite Majesty. Yes, you should revere him and humble yourself before him—especially when you call to mind the ingratitude and the outrages you have been guilty of in the past.

But this should not hinder you from speaking with him with the most tender love and confidence you can. He is Infinite Majesty, but at the same time, he is Infinite Goodness and Infinite Love.

In God you possess the Lord most exalted and supreme, but you also have him who loves you with the greatest possible love. He delights that you should enjoy with him the same confidence, freedom, and tenderness that children enjoy with their mothers. Hear how he invites us to come to his feet and of the caresses he promises to give us: *You shall be carried at the breasts, and upon the knees they shall caress you. As one whom the mother caresseth, so will I comfort you* (Isaiah 66:12-13, Douay). As a mother delights to place her little child upon her knees and feed or caress him, so does our gracious God, with similar tenderness, delight to treat those he loves, those who have given themselves wholly to him and placed all their hopes in his goodness.

To strengthen your confidence in God, often call to mind his loving treatment of you and the gracious means he has used to drive you from the disorders of your life and your attachments to earth in order to draw you to his holy love. Therefore, you should fear having too little confidence in speaking with your God now that you have resolved to love and to please him with all your power. The mercies he has granted you are most sure pledges of the love he has for you. God is displeased with a lack of trust on the part of those who heartily love him and whom he

loves. So if you desire to please his loving heart, converse with him from this day forward with the greatest confidence and tenderness you possibly can. ∾

The Way of Salvation and of Perfection

DOES JESUS ASK TOO MUCH OF US?

Does Jesus Christ, perhaps, claim too much in wanting us to give ourselves entirely to him after he has given to us all his blood and his life in dying for us upon the cross? *For the love of Christ controls us* (2 Corinthians 5:14). Let us hear what St. Francis de Sales says: "To know that Jesus has loved us to the point of death—and even the death on the cross—isn't this to feel our hearts constrained by a violence that is that much stronger because of its loveliness?" And then he adds, "My Jesus gives himself all to me, and I give myself all to him. On his bosom will I live and die. Neither death nor life shall ever separate me from him."

It was for this end, St. Paul says, that Jesus Christ died, that each of us should no longer live to the world nor to himself, but to him alone who has given himself wholly to us. *And he died for all, that those who live might live no longer for themselves but for him who for their sake died* (2 Corinthians 5:15). He who lives for the world seeks to please the world; he who lives to Jesus Christ seeks only to please Jesus Christ and fears only to displease him. His only joy is to see him loved; his only sorrow, to see him despised. This is to live for Jesus Christ, and this is what he claims from each one of us. I repeat, does he claim too much from us, after having given us his blood and his life?

Why, then, O my God, do we spend our affections on loving creatures, relatives, friends, and the great ones of the world, who have never suffered scourges, thorns, or nails, nor shed one drop of blood for us, instead of on loving God, who for love of us came down from heaven and was made man, shed all his blood for us in the midst of torments, and finally died of grief upon a cross in order to win our hearts to himself! And, in order to unite himself more closely to us, he has left himself after his death upon our altars, where he makes himself one with us so that we might understand how burning is the love with which he loves us. "He has mingled himself with us," exclaims St. John Chrysostom, "that we may be one and the same thing, for this is the desire of those who ardently love."

The Way of Salvation and of Perfection

THE DEAREST FRIEND YOU HAVE

I *have graven you on the palms of my hands; your walls are continually before me* (Isaiah 49:16). "Beloved soul," says the Lord, "what do you fear or mistrust? You are written in my hands, so I will never forget to do you good. Are you afraid of your enemies? Know that the care of your defense is always before me so that I cannot lose sight of it." Therefore David rejoiced, saying to God, *Thou dost cover him with favor as with a shield* (Psalm 5:12).

Who, O Lord, can ever harm us, if you with your goodness and love defend and surround us? Above all, strengthen your confidence at the thought of the gift that God has given us in Jesus Christ: *For God so loved the world that he gave his only Son* (John 3:16). How can we ever fear, exclaims the Apostle Paul, that God would refuse to do us good after he has promised to give us his own Son? *He who did not spare his own Son but gave him up for us all, will he not also give us all things with him?* (Romans 8:32).

My delights were to be with the children of men (Proverbs 8:31, Douay). The heart of man is God's paradise, so to speak. Does God love you? Love him. His delights are to be with you: Let your delight be to be with him, to pass all your lifetime with him, in the delight of whose company you hope to spend a blissful eternity. Accustom yourself to speak with him alone, familiarly, with confidence and love, as to the dearest friend you have and the one who loves you best. ❧

The Way of Salvation and of Perfection

CONSIDER THE SUFFERINGS OF MARY

Who can ever have a heart so hard that it would not melt on hearing the most sorrowful event that ever occurred in the world? There was a noble and holy mother who had an only son. He was the most wonderful son you can imagine—innocent, virtuous, beautiful. He loved his mother most tenderly, so much so that he never caused her the least displeasure, but always showed her all respect, obedience, and affection. Therefore, this mother had placed all her earthly affection on this son. Hear what happened then. This son was falsely accused by his enemies out of envy, and though the judge knew—and even confessed—that the son was innocent, still, in order not to offend his own enemies, he condemned him to the horrible death they demanded. This poor mother had to suffer the grief of seeing her kind and beloved son unjustly snatched from her by a barbaric death. Being tormented and drained of all his blood, he was made to die on an infamous cross in a public place of execution, and all this happened before her own eyes. What do you say? Isn't this event, isn't this un-happy mother, worthy of compassion?

You already know of whom I speak. This son, so cruelly executed, was our loving Redeemer, Jesus, and this mother was the Blessed Virgin Mary. For the love she has for us, was willing to see him sacrificed for the sake of God's justice by the barbarity of men. This great torment Mary endured for us—a torment that was more than a thousand deaths—deserves both our compassion and our gratitude. If we can make no other return for so much love, at least let us give a few moments this day to consider the greatness of the sufferings by which Mary became the Queen of Martyrs. ❧

The Glories of Mary

WRITE YOUR NAME ON MY HEART

The name of Jesus was given to the Incarnate Word not by men, but by God himself: *And you shall call his name Jesus* (Luke 1:31), that is, *Savior*, a name of glad-ness, a name of hope, a name of love.

A name of *gladness*, because if remembering our past sins afflicts us, this name comforts us, reminding us that the Son of God became man for this purpose, to make himself our Savior. . . .

A name of *hope*, because he who prays to the Eternal Father in the name of Jesus may hope for every grace he asks for: *If you ask anything of the Father, he will give it to you in my name* (John 16:23). . . .

A name of *love* because, as St. Bernardine of Siena says, the name of Jesus is a sign that represents to us how much God has done for the love of us.

O my Jesus! I beg you, write your name on my poor heart and on my tongue so that when I am tempted to sin, I may resist by calling on you. And so if I am tempted to despair, I may trust in your grace, and if I feel lukewarm in my love for you, your name may inflame my heart with the recollection of how much you have loved me. ❧

The Incarnation, Birth and Infancy of Jesus Christ

WHAT ELSE DO I DESIRE?

O love of my soul, most Holy Sacrament! I wish that I could always remember you and forget everything else, and that I could love you alone, without interruption and without reserve! Ah, Jesus, you have knocked at the door of my heart so frequently that I hope at last you have entered in. But since you have entered there, I pray that you drive away all its affections that do not tend towards you. Possess me entirely for yourself so that

I may be able to say to you in truth from this day forward, *Whom have I in heaven but thee? And there is nothing upon earth that I desire besides thee. My flesh and my heart may fail, but God is the strength of my heart and my portion for ever* (Psalm 73:25-26). Yes, O my God, what else do I desire on earth or in heaven but you? You alone are and will always be the only Lord of my heart and my will. You alone will be all my portion and all my riches in this life and in the next. ∾

The Passion and the Death of Jesus Christ

8

Embracing God's Will

In all that happens to me,
whether it is pleasant or painful,
I receive it from God's hands with joy
as being what is best for me.
In this lies my happiness.

The True Spouse of Jesus Christ

LORD, TAKE POSSESSION OF ME

Jesus Christ has taught us to pray so that we may perform the divine will on earth as the saints perform it in heaven: *Thy will be done, on earth as it is in heaven* (Matthew 6:10). The Lord calls David a man after his own heart because David accomplished all his desires: *I have found in David the son of Jesse a man after my heart, who will do all my will* (Acts 13:22). David was always prepared to embrace God's will, as he frequently declared: *My heart is steadfast, O God, my heart is steadfast* (Psalm 108:1). And he prayed that the Lord would teach him to do his will: *Teach me to do thy will* (Psalm 143:10). A single act of perfect conformity to the divine will is sufficient to make one a saint.

Look at Saul, whom Jesus Christ illuminates and converts while he is continuing his persecution of the church. What does Saul do? What does he say? He simply makes an offering of himself to do God's will: *Lord, what wilt thou have me to do?* (Acts 9:6, Douay). And, behold, the Lord declares: *He is a chosen instrument of mine to carry my name before the Gentiles* (Acts 9:15).

Yes, for he who gives his will to God gives him everything. Now he who gives God his goods in alms, his blood by disciplines, and his food by fasting, gives to God a part of what he possesses. But he who gives him his will gives him everything so he can say to him, "Lord, I am poor, but I give you all that is in my power: There remains nothing for me to give you." This is precisely all that our God claims from us: *My son, give me your heart* (Proverbs 23:26). "My son," says the Lord to each of us, "My son, give me your heart," that is to say, your will. "There is no offering," says St. Augustine, "that we can make to God more acceptable than to say to him, 'Take possession of us.'" No, we cannot offer to God anything more precious than to say to him, "We give our whole will to you. Make us understand what it is you desire of us and we will perform it." ❧

The Way of Salvation and of Perfection

CAST YOUR CARES UPON HIM

God has the greatest desire to make the souls of men partakers of his own bliss and glory. And if in this life he sends us trials, they are all for our own good: *We know that in everything God works for good* (Romans 8:28). . . .

In order to save us from eternal evils, the Lord throws his own good will around us: *O LORD; thou dost cover him with favor as with a shield* (Psalm 5:12). He not only desires but is anxious for our salvation: *The Lord takes thought for me* (Psalm 40:17). And what is there that God will ever refuse us, asks St. Paul, after having given us his own Son? *He who did not spare his own Son but gave him up for us all, will he not also give us all things with him?* (Romans 8:32). Then this is the confidence with which we ought to abandon ourselves to God's will, which has as its purpose our own good. Let us always say, under all the circumstances that happen to us, *In peace I will both lie down and sleep; for thou alone, O LORD, makest me dwell in safety* (Psalm 4:8). Let us also place ourselves entirely in his hands, for he will certainly take care of us: *Cast all your anxieties on him, for he cares about you* (1 Peter 5:7). ❧

The Way of Salvation and of Perfection

CONTENT IN GOD'S WILL

If we have any natural defect, either in mind or body—a bad memory, slowness in comprehension, limited abilities, a disabled limb, or weak health—let's not complain. What was it that we deserved and what obligation did God have to give us a mind more richly endowed or a body more perfectly framed? Could he not have created us mere brute animals? Or have left us in our own nothingness? Who ever receives a gift and tries to make bargains about it? Let us then return him thanks for what, through a pure act of his goodness, he has given us. Let us be content with the manner in which he has treated us. Who can tell whether, if we had had a larger share of ability, stronger health, or greater personal attractions, we should have not used them to our destruction? How many people have come to ruin because they have been proud of their talents and learning and, as a result, have looked on others with contempt—a danger that can easily happen to those who exceed others in learning and ability! And there are many others whose personal beauty or bodily strength have provided the occasions that have plunged them into innumerable acts of wickedness! On the contrary, how many others there are who, as a result of their poverty, or infirmity, or unattractiveness, have sanctified themselves and been saved. And so let us be content with what God has given us: *One thing is needful* (Luke 10:42). Beauty is not necessary, nor health, nor sharpness of intellect. That which alone is necessary is our salvation.

Our Physical Infirmities. We must be resigned to embrace physical infirmities willingly, both in such a way and for such a time as God wills. Nevertheless, we should employ the usual remedies, for this is what the Lord wills also. But if they do us no good, let us unite ourselves to the will of God. This will do us much more good than health. Let us then say, "O Lord, I have no wish either to get well or to remain sick: I want only what you will." Certainly the virtue is greater if, in times of sickness, we do not complain about our sufferings. But when these press heavily upon us, it is not a fault to make them known to our friends, or even to pray to God to liberate us from them. I am speaking now of severe sufferings. On the other hand, there are many who are at fault in that, with every trifling pain or weariness, they want the whole world to have compassion on them and to shed tears around them.

Even Jesus Christ, when he was nearing the time of his most bitter Passion, manifested to his disciples what he suffered: *My soul is very sorrowful, even to death* (Matthew 26:38), and he prayed that the Eternal Father would free him from it: *My Father, if it be possible, let this cup pass from me* (26:39). But Jesus himself taught us what we ought to do after praying—namely, to immediately resign ourselves to God's will, by adding, as he did, *Nevertheless, not as I will, but as thou wilt* (26:39).

Loss of Meaningful People. We must also accept the loss we suffer at times regarding people who, from either a temporal or spiritual point of view, happen to be of importance to us. This is often a fault of those who are devout, because they are not willing to resign God-given comforts. Our sanctification must come not from spiritual directors, but from God. Yes, it is his will that we should avail ourselves of directors as spiritual guides when he gives them to us, but when he takes them away, he wants us to rest content and increase our confidence in his goodness, saying at such times, "Lord, it is you who has given me this assistance; now you have taken it from me. May your will be always done. But I pray that you will supply my wants, and teach me what I ought to do to serve you." And we ought to receive all other crosses from the hands of God in the same way. But so many troubles, you say, are chastisements. I ask in reply, are not the chastisements that God sends us in this life acts of kindness and benefits? . . .

So, when suffering the chastisements of God, let us say what was said by the high priest: *It is the Lord; let him do what seems good to him* (1 Samuel 3:18).

Spiritual Desolation. When a person commits himself to the spiritual life, the Lord often sends many comforts to him in order to wean him from the pleasures of the world. But afterward, when he sees that the person is more settled in spiritual ways, he draws back his hand in order to test his love and to see whether he serves and loves without reward while in this world with spiritual joy. "While we are living here," St. Teresa used to say, "Our gain is not found in enjoying God more, but in performing his will." And in another passage: "The love of God does not consist in tenderness, but in serving him with firmness and humility." And again, elsewhere: "The Lord makes trial of those who love him by means of drynesses and temptations." So then let the person thank the Lord when he caresses him with sweetnesses, but not torment himself by acts of impatience when he feels himself desolate.

This is a point to which you should pay close attention because some foolish people, seeing themselves in a state of aridity, think that God may have abandoned them or that the spiritual life was not made for them, and so they quit praying and lose all they have gained. There is no time better for exercising our resignation to the will of God than during a time of dryness. I am not saying that being without the perceptible presence of your God will not cause you pain. It is impossible for a person not to feel pain or not to be sorrowful when our Redeemer himself upon the cross was sorrowful for this very reason: *My God, my God, why hast thou forsaken me?* (Matthew 27:46). But, in our sufferings, we should always resign ourselves perfectly to the will of our Lord. These spiritual desolations and abandonments are what all the saints have suffered. "What hardness of heart," said St. Bernard, "do I not experience! I no longer find any delight in reading, no longer any pleasure in meditation or in prayer." The condition of the saints has been ordinarily one of dryness, not of perceptible comforts. These are things that the Lord does not grant, except on rare occasions, and to perhaps weaker people in order to prevent their coming to a standstill in their spiritual journey. The joys that are meant to be our rewards he prepares for us in Paradise. ❧

The Way of Salvation and of Perfection

THE BAREFOOTED BEGGAR

Father John Taulerus relates that after having prayed to the Lord for many years to send someone to instruct him in the true spiritual life, he heard a voice one day saying to him, "Go to such-and-such church and you will find what you ask for." On reaching the church, he found at the gate a beggar, barefooted and with scarcely a rag on his back. He saluted him: "Good day, my friend."

The poor man replied, "Sir, I do not remember ever having a happy life, but I have never been unhappy." And then he went on to say: "Listen, my Father, it is not without reason I've told you that when I suffer hunger, I praise God; when it snows or rains, I bless him; if I am treated with contempt or rejected by anyone, or if I experience misfortunes of any kind, I always give glory to God for it. I also told you I have never been unhappy, and this is true because it is my habit to desire, without reservation, all that God desires. Therefore, in all that happens to me, whether it is pleasant or painful, I receive it from his hands with joy as being what is best for me. In this lies my happiness."

"And if it should ever happen," said Taulerus, "that God willed you to be damned, what would you say then?"

"If God were to will this," replied the beggar, "I would, with all humility and love, lock myself so fast in my Lord's embrace and hold him so tight that if it were his will to cast me down into hell, he would have to come along with me. So with him, it would be sweeter for me to be in hell than to possess without him all the enjoyments of heaven."

"Where was it you found God?" asked the Father.

"I found him when I took leave of creatures," was the reply.

"Who are you?"

The poor man answered, "I am a king. And when everything is in due order, the passions are subjected to the reason, and the reason to God."

In conclusion, Taulerus asked him what it was that had inspired him on to so high a degree of perfection. "It has been silence," he said. "Observing silence with man in order to hold conversation with God, and also union with God's will."

Certainly this man was, in all his poverty, wealthier than all the monarchs of the earth, and in his sufferings happier than all the men of the world with their earthly pleasures. ❧

The Way of Salvation and of Perfection

CONFORMITY IN ALL THINGS

Our primary goal lies in our embracing the will of God in all things that happen to us, not only when they are favorable but also when they are contrary to our desires. When things go well, even sinners find no difficulty conforming to God's will. But the saints are in conformity even under circumstances that run counter to their desires and crush their self-love. It is in this that the perfection of our love for God is shown. The Venerable Father John of Avila used to say, "A single 'Blessed be God' when things are going wrong is of more value than thousands of thanksgivings when they are to our liking."

What's more, we must bring ourselves into conformity to the divine will not only in those adverse circumstances that come to us directly from God—for instance, illness, desolations of spirit, poverty, the death of parents, and other things of a similar nature—but also regarding those difficulties that come to us through the actions of men, as in the case of haughtiness, contempt, reproaches, acts of injustice, thefts, and persecutions of every kind. On this point, we must understand that when we suffer injury from anyone, whether in our reputation, our honor, or our property, although the Lord does not will the sin that such a person commits, he nevertheless does will our humiliation, our poverty, and our mortification.

It is certain and a foundation of our faith that everything that comes to pass in the world comes to pass through the divine will: *I form the light and create darkness. I make peace and create evil* (Isaiah 45:7, Douay). From God comes all things that are good and all things that are evil—that is to say, all things that are contrary to our own liking and that we falsely call evil for, in truth, they are good when we receive them as coming from his hands: *Does evil befall a city, unless the LORD has done it?* (Amos 3:6) said the prophet Amos. And the wise man said it before that: *Good things and bad, life and death, poverty and wealth, come from the Lord* (Sirach 11:14). ❧

The Way of Salvation and of Perfection

9

Preparing for Eternity

O time misused during life!
People in the world will ardently desire
you at the hour of death!
They will then wish for another year,
another month, another day,
but they will not obtain it.

Preparation for Death

THE CERTAINTY OF DEATH

The sentence of death has been written against all men: You are a man and you must die. "Our other goods and evils are uncertain; death alone is certain," says St. Augustine. It is uncertain whether the infant that is just born will be poor or rich, whether he will have good or bad health, whether he will die in youth or in old age. But it is certain that he will die. The stroke of death will fall on all the nobles and monarchs of the earth. When death comes, there is no earthly power able to resist it. St. Augustine says, "Fire, water, the sword, and the power of princes may be resisted, but death cannot be resisted."

At the end of his life a certain king of France said: "Behold, with all my power I cannot convince death to wait one more hour for me." When the term of life arrives, it is not deferred a single moment. *Thou hast appointed his bounds that he cannot pass* (Job 14:5).

Dearly beloved reader, though you should live as many years as you expect, a day will come, and on that day an hour that will be the last for you. For me, who is now writing, and for you, who are reading this little book, there has been decreed the day and the moment when I will no longer write and you will no longer read. *What man can live and never see death?* (Psalm 89:48). The sentence has been already passed. There never has been a man so foolish as to flatter himself that he will not have to die. What has happened to your forefathers will also happen to you. Of the immense number of people who lived in this country in the beginning of the last century, there is not one now living. Even the princes and monarchs of the earth have changed their country. Of them nothing now remains but a marble mausoleum with a grand inscription, which only serves to teach us that of the great ones of the world nothing is left but a little dust enclosed in the tomb. "Tell me," says Bernard, "where are those who love this world? Of them nothing remains except ashes and worms."

Since our souls will be eternal, we ought to take hold of a fortune that will be everlasting, not one that soon ends. What would it profit you to be happy here (if it were possible for a soul to be happy without God) if after this you must be miserable for all eternity? You have built that house to your entire satisfaction, but remember that you must soon leave it to rot in a grave. You have obtained that dignity which raises you above others, but death will come and reduce you to the level of the poorest peasant. ∾

Preparation for Death

A FOOLISH TRAVELER

What foolishness it would be for a traveler to think only of acquiring dignities and possessions in the countries he was passing through, then live miserably in his native land where he must remain his whole life! And is he not a fool who seeks after happiness in this world, where he will remain only a few days, and exposes himself to the risk of being unhappy in the next, where he must live for eternity? We do not fix our affections on borrowed goods because we know they must soon be returned to the owner. Likewise, all the goods of this earth are lent to us: It is folly to set our heart on what we must soon give up. Death shall strip us of them all. The acquisitions and fortunes of this world all terminate in a dying gasp, in a funeral, in a descent into the grave. The house you have built for yourself you must soon give up to others. The grave will be the dwelling of your body till the day of judgment; then it will go to heaven or to hell, where your soul will have gone before. ❧

Preparation for Death

Don't View Death at a Distance

All know they must die: But the misfortune is, many view death at such a distance that they lose sight of it. Even the old, the most feeble, and the most sickly flatter themselves by thinking they will live three or four years longer. But how many, I ask, have we known, even in our own times, to die suddenly—some sitting, some walking, some sleeping? It is certain that none of these imagined he would die so suddenly or on that day on which he died. What's more, of all who have gone to the other world during the present year, no one imagined he would die and end his days this year. Few are the deaths that do not happen unexpectedly.

Therefore, Christian soul, when the devil tempts you to sin by saying, "Tomorrow you will go to confession," let your answer be, "How do I know that this will not be the last day of my life? If this hour, this moment, in which I would turn my back on God were the last of my life, I would have no time for repentance and what would become of me for all eternity?" The devil tells you that this misfortune will not happen to you, but you should answer him: "If it should happen to me, what will become of me for all eternity?" ❧

Preparation for Death

AMEND YOUR LIFE NOW

The Lord does not wish us to be lost. Therefore by threatening to chastise us, he unceasingly encourages us to a change of life. *Except you will be converted, he will brandish his sword* (Psalm 7:13, Douay). In another place, he says: How many, because they would not stop offending me, have met with a sudden death when they were least expecting it and were living in peace, thinking they had many years left? *When people say, "There is peace and security," then sudden destruction will come upon them* (1 Thessalonians 5:3). Again he says: *Unless you repent you will all likewise perish* (Luke 13:5). Why so many threats of chastisement before the execution of vengeance? It is because the Lord wishes that we amend our lives and thus avoid an unhappy death. "He who tells you to beware does not wish to take away your life," says St. Augustine.

It is necessary, then, to prepare our accounts before the day of account arrives. Dearly beloved Christians, if you were to die and your fate for eternity were to be decided before nightfall, would you be ready? How much would you give to obtain from God another year or month, or even another day, to prepare for judgment? Then why don't you—now that God gives you this time—settle the accounts of your conscience? Do you think, perhaps, that it cannot happen that this will be the last day for you? *Do not delay to turn to the Lord, nor postpone it from day to day; for suddenly the wrath of the Lord will go forth, and at the time of punishment you will perish* (Sirach 5:7).

My brother, to save your soul you must give up sin. "If then you must renounce it at some time, why do you not abandon it at this moment?" asks St. Augustine. ∽

Preparation for Death

SETTLE YOUR ACCOUNTS

Brother, since it is certain you will die, go as soon as possible to the foot of the crucifix. Thank your crucified Redeemer for the time which in his mercy he gives you to settle the affairs of your conscience and then review all the irregularities of your past life, particularly of your youth. Cast a glance at the commandments of God. Examine yourself regarding the duties of the state of life you have lived, and regarding the society you have frequented. Write down the sins you have committed. Make a general confession of your whole life, if you have not as yet made one. O! How much good a general confession contributes to the life of a Christian! Think about how you have to settle accounts for eternity and take care to adjust them as if you were on the point of rendering these accounts to Jesus Christ at judgment. Banish from your heart every sinful affection and every sentiment of rancor. . . . Resolve to fly from all those occasions in which you should be in danger of losing God. Remember that what now seems difficult will appear impossible at the hour of death.

It is still more important for you to resolve to practice the means of preserving your soul in the grace of God. These means are hearing Mass every day, meditating on the eternal truths, frequenting of the sacraments of Penance and the Eucharist. . . . And as to the past, trust in the blood of Jesus Christ, who now gives you enlightenment because he desires your salvation. And trust in the intercession of Mary, who obtains enlightenment for you. If you adopt this mode of life and place great confidence in Jesus and Mary, what aid will you receive from God and what strength will your soul acquire!

Dearly beloved reader, give yourself now to God who invites you, and begin to enjoy that peace you have been deprived of through your own fault until now. And what greater peace can a soul enjoy than to be able to say in going to rest at night: "Should death come this night, I hope to die in the grace of God!" How happy the man who, amid the terrors of thunder or of earthquakes, is prepared to accept death with resignation should God be pleased to send it! ❧

Preparation for Death

Nothing Is More Precious Than Time

There is nothing more precious than time, but there is nothing less valued and more misused by men of the world. This is what St. Bernard deplores when he says: "Nothing is more precious than time, but nothing is regarded more cheaply." The same saint adds: "The days of salvation pass away, and no one reflects that the day which has passed away from him can never return." You will see a gambler spend nights and days in play. If you ask him what he is doing, his answer is: "I am passing the time." You will see others standing several hours in the street, looking at those who pass by, and speaking about obscene or useless subjects. If you ask them what they are doing, they will say: "We are passing the time." Poor blind sinners, who lose so many days that will never return.

O time misused during life! People in the world will ardently desire you at the hour of death! They will then wish for another year, another month, another day, but they will not obtain it. . . . .

The prophet exhorts us to remember God and to procure his friendship before the light fails. *Remember also your Creator . . . before the sun and the light . . . are darkened* (Ecclesiastes 12:1-2). How great is the distress and misery of a traveler who, when the night has come, realizes that he has missed the way and that there is no time to correct the mistake. Such will be the anguish at death of the sinner who has lived many years in the world and has not spent them for God. *Night comes, when no one can work* (John 9:4). For him, death shall be the night in which he will be able to do nothing. *He hath called against me the time* (Lamentations 1:15, Douay).

Conscience will then remind the man of the world of all the time God gave him that he has spent in the destruction of his soul, of all the calls and graces he has received from God for his sanctification that he has voluntarily abused. The sinner will then see that the way of salvation is closed forever. Then he will weep and say: "I have been a fool! O time lost! O life misspent! O lost years, in which I could have, but have not, become a saint! And now the time of salvation is gone forever." But of what use are these sighs and cries, when the scene is about to close—the lamp at the point of being extinguished—and when the dying sinner has reached that awful moment on which eternity depends? ∞

Preparation for Death

WALK WHILE YOU HAVE THE LIGHT

W*alk while you have the light* (John 12:35). We must walk in the way of the Lord during life, now that we have light, for at the hour of death this light is taken away. Death is not the time for preparing, but for finding ourselves prepared. Be ready. At the hour of death we can do nothing: Then, what is done is done. O God! If a person were told that in a short time a trial would take place on which his life and his entire property would depend, with what haste would he seek an able lawyer to plead his cause! How little time would he lose in adopting every means of securing a favorable result! And what are we doing? We know for certain that the most important of all causes—the affair of eternal salvation—will soon be decided. The decision may take place any hour, and still we lose time.

Some may say: "I am young; I will give myself to God later." But remember that, as the Gospel remarks, the Lord cursed the fig tree the first time he found it without fruit, although the season for figs had not arrived. By this Jesus Christ wished to show us that men should at all times, even in their youth, bring forth fruits of good works. Otherwise they will be accursed, and will never more bring forth fruit. *May no one ever eat fruit from you again* (Mark 11:14). Such is the curse of the Redeemer on the fruitless fig tree; such is his curse against all who resist his calls. Satan regards the whole time of our life as short, and therefore he does not lose a moment in tempting us. *The devil has come down to you in great wrath, because he knows that his time is short!* (Revelation 12:12). If even the devil loses no time in seeking our damnation, shall we lose the time given to us to secure our salvation?

Some will say, "What evil am I doing?" O God, is it not an evil to lose time in gaming, in useless conversations, which are unprofitable to the soul? Does God give you time that you may squander it? No: the Holy Spirit says, *Do not deprive yourself of a happy day; let not your share of desired good pass by you* (Sirach 14:14). The workmen who are mentioned by St. Matthew, though they did no evil except to lose time, were rebuked by the master of the vineyard. *Why do you stand here idle all day?* (Matthew 20:6). On the day of judgment Jesus Christ will demand an account of every idle word. All the time that is not spent for God is lost, all the time in which you have not thought of God. Therefore, the Holy Spirit says, *Whatever your hand finds to do, do it with your might; for there is no work or thought or knowledge or wisdom in Sheol, to which you are going* (Ecclesiastes 9:10). The Venerable Sister Jane of the Most Holy Trinity, of the Order of St. Teresa, used to say that in the lives of the saints there is no tomorrow. Tomorrow is found in the lives of sinners, who always say, "Later, later," and in this state they continue until death. *Behold, now is the acceptable time* (2 Corinthians 6:2). *O that today you would hearken to his voice! Harden not your hearts* (Psalm 95:7-8). If God calls you today to do good, do it, for tomorrow it may happen that your time will be no more, or that God will call you no more. ⧆

Preparation for Death

THE CHOICE RESTS WITH US

God wills the salvation of all men, but he will not save us by force. He has placed before each of us life and death—whichever we choose will be given us. The Lord has given us two ways in which to walk: one the way of heaven, the other the way of hell. Before a man are life and death, and whichever he chooses will be given to him (Sirach 15:17). The choice rests with us. . . .

Let us not be foolish. Let us reflect that eternity is at stake. In erecting a house in which he expects to live for the remainder of his life, a man spares no trouble in seeking a healthful site, and submits to great toil and fatigue in endeavoring to make the house accommodating and airy. Then why are men so careless when there is question of the house in which they must dwell for eternity? The business for which we labor, says St. Eucherius, is eternity. This is not a question of a house being more or less accommodating or more or less airy. This is a question of being in a place full of delights among the friends of God, or in a pit of all torments in the midst of an infamous crowd of abandoned criminals. And for how long? Not for twenty or forty years, but for all eternity. This is a great point. It is not a business of little moment; it is an affair of infinite importance. ❧

Preparation for Death

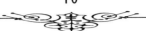

10

Living for God

Holy desires are the blessed wings
with which the saints break every worldly tie
and fly to the mountain of perfection,
where they find that peace
which the world cannot give.

The True Spouse of Jesus Christ

THE LORD AS YOUR SPOUSE

In the parable of the virgins, Jesus himself wished to be called their spouse: *Then the kingdom of heaven shall be compared to ten maidens who took their lamps and went to meet the bridegroom* (Matthew 25:1). St. Bernard assured us that all just souls are spouses of the Lord.

Let us then ask the spouse we find in the Song of Solomon, who is this divine bridegroom? Tell me, what are the qualities of your beloved, the only object of your affection, who makes you the happiest of

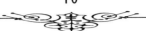

women? *What manner of one is thy beloved of the beloved, O thou most beautiful among women?* (Canticles 5:9, Douay). She will answer: *My beloved is radiant and ruddy, distinguished among ten thousand* (5:10). My beloved is made white by his innocence, and ruddy by the ardor with which he loves his spouses. In a word, he is so loving, so perfect in all virtues, and at the same time so courteous and affable, that he is of all spouses the most dear and amiable. St. Eucherius says, "There is nothing more glorious, nothing more beautiful, nothing more magnificent, than he is." ∾

The True Spouse of Jesus Christ

THE WAY OF PERFECTION

Just as to hit a bird in flight the sportsman must take aim in advance of his prey, so a Christian, to make progress in virtue, should aspire to the highest degree of holiness in his power to attain.

St. Gregory beautifully explains this maxim of spiritual life by comparing a Christian who seeks to remain stationary in the path of virtue to a man who is in a boat on a rapid river, striving to keep the boat always in the same position. If the boat is not continually propelled against the current, it will be carried away in an opposite direction.

In seeking eternal salvation we must, according to St. Paul, never rest but must run continually in the way of perfection, that we may win the prize and secure an incorruptible crown. *So run that you may obtain it* (1 Corinthians 9:24). If we fail, the fault will be ours, for God wills that all are holy and perfect. *For this is the will of God, your sanctification* (1 Thessalonians 4:3). He even commands us to be perfect and holy. *You, therefore, must be perfect, as your heavenly Father is perfect* (Matthew 5:48). *Be holy, for I am holy* (Leviticus 11:44). He promises and gives, as the holy Council of Trent teaches, abundant strength for the observance of all his commands to those who ask it from him.

God does not command impossibilities, but by his precepts he urges us to do what we can by the aid of his ordinary grace, and when greater helps are necessary, he encourages us to seek them by humble prayer. He will without fail respond to our requests and enable us to observe even the most difficult of his commandments. Take courage, then, and adopt the advice of the Venerable Father Torres to one of his penitents: "Let us, my child, put on the wings of strong desires, that, quitting the earth, we may fly to our Spouse and our Beloved, who expects us in the blessed kingdom of eternity." ❧

The True Spouse of Jesus Christ

TRUE GLORY

Seeing the world covered with the toils of the devil, St. Anthony with a sigh exclaimed: "Who can escape so many snares!" "Anthony," replied a strange voice, "it is only the humble who pass through them with security: The humble man is not in danger of being caught by them." In a word, unless we are like infants, not in years but in humility, we shall never attain salvation. *Unless you turn and become like children, you will never enter the kingdom of heaven* (Matthew 18:3). . . . To the humble who are despised and persecuted on earth is promised the glory of God's kingdom. *Blessed are you when men revile you and persecute you . . . for your reward is great in heaven* (5:11-12). The humble shall be happy in this life as well as in the next. *Learn from me; for I am gentle and lowly in heart, and you will find rest for your souls* (11:29).

The proud never enjoy peace because they never receive the respect or attention that a vain opinion of their own greatness makes them think is their due. When loaded with honors, they are not content, either because they see others even more exalted or because they desire some unattainable dignity, the absence of which is a source of torture to them that is not removed by all the honors they enjoy. Great indeed was the glory of Haman in the court of King Ahasuerus, where he sat at the monarch's table. But, because Mordecai would not salute him, he was unhappy. *Yet all this does me no good, so long as I see Mordecai the Jew sitting at the king's gate* (Esther 5:13). Because it is often the outcome of being forced to show human respect, the honor shown to the great does not give true joy. "True glory," says St. Jerome, "like a shadow, follows virtue: It flies from all who grasp at it, and seeks after those who despise it." ❧

The True Spouse of Jesus Christ

TRUE HUMILITY

Some imagine, says St. Francis of Assisi, that sanctity consists in the recital of many prayers or in the performance of works of penance. But, not understanding how much can be gained by bearing insults patiently, these same people cannot bear an injurious word. It is better to meekly receive an affront than fast ten days on bread and water. It will sometimes happen that a privilege refused to you will be given to others; that what you say will be treated with contempt, while the words of others are heard with respectful attention; that while the actions of others are the theme of general praise and they are elected to the offices of honor, you are passed by unnoticed and your whole conduct is made a subject of derision. If you accept in peace all these humiliations and if, with a brotherly or sisterly affection, you recommend to God those from whom you receive the least respect, then indeed, as St. Dorotheus says, it will be clear that you are truly humble. To these people you are particularly indebted, since by their actions they cure your pride—the most malignant of all diseases that leads to spiritual death. Because they consider themselves worthy of all honors, the proud convert even their humiliations into an occasion of pride. But because the humble consider themselves deserving only of insult, their humiliations serve to increase their humility. "That man is truly humble," says St. Bernard, "who converts humiliation into humility." ❧

The True Spouse of Jesus Christ

CHARITY

Take care always to speak well of all. Speak of others as you would wish to be spoken of by others. With regard to the absent, observe the excellent rule of St. Mary Magdalene de Pazzi: "Never utter in their absence what you would not say in their presence." And if you ever hear a sister speak ill of others, be careful neither to encourage her uncharitableness nor to appear pleased with her language. Otherwise, you will partake of her guilt. You should either reprove her, or change the subject of conversation, or withdraw from her, or at least pay no attention to her. *See that you fence in your property with thorns . . . make balances and scales for your words* (Sirach 28:24-25).

Take care to protect your ears from hearing criticism, so it may not enter. Whenever you hear a person speak ill of others, it is necessary to show—at least by silence, by a gloomy expression, or by downcast eyes—that you are not pleased with the conversation. Conduct yourself always in such a way that no one in the future will dare attack the character of another in your presence. And when it is in your power, charity requires you to take the part of the person who is criticized. ❧

The True Spouse of Jesus Christ

PATIENCE IN SUFFERING

Y ou should thank God when he chastises you, for his chastisements are a proof that he loves you and receives you into the number of his children. *For the Lord disciplines him whom he loves*, says St. Paul, *and chastises every son whom he receives* (Hebrews 12:6). Therefore, St.

Augustine says: "Do you enjoy consolation? Acknowledge a father who caresses you. Are you in tribulation? Recognize a parent who corrects you." In the future, when you find yourself in tribulation, do not say that God has forgotten you. Say rather that you have forgotten your sins. He who knows he has offended God must pray with St. Bonaventure: "Run, O Lord, run, and wound your servants with sacred wounds, lest they be wounded with the wounds of death." ❧

The True Spouse of Jesus Christ

CONTENTMENT

What would you think of a beggar who complains that the garment you give him is not as rich as he would like, or that the food is not as delicious as he desires? Let us, then, be content with what God has given us and seek nothing else. Could he not have left us in our nothingness? Could he not ordain that, instead of being men, we should be toads, flies, or blades of grass? Oh how often has the lack of mental acuteness, of physical beauty, or of other natural gifts contributed to the salvation of many! For many, the possession of such qualifications might be the occasion of their damnation. To how many have great talents—beauty, nobility, and wealth—been the cause of pride and haughtiness and of running headlong into a multitude of crimes? Let us, then, desire only the goods God wishes to give us, and no more. And though we ought to aspire to the highest sanctity we can attain, we should be content with that degree of perfection that God gives us. ❧

The True Spouse of Jesus Christ

OUR SOUL, GOD'S DWELLING

The kings of the earth, though they have their great palaces, usually have their particular apartments in which they live. Likewise, God is in all places and his presence fills heaven and earth, but he dwells in a particular manner in our souls. There, as he tells us through the Apostle John, he delights to remain, as in so many gardens of pleasure: *I will live in them and move among them, and I will be their God* (2 Corinthians 6:16). There he wishes us to love him and to pray to him, for he remains in us full of love and mercy, to hear our requests, to receive our affections, to enlighten us, to govern us, to give us his gifts, and to assist us in all that can contribute to our eternal salvation.

Let us then often resolve, on the one hand, to enliven our faith in this great truth and to humble ourselves at the sight of the great majesty that has come down to dwell within. On the other, let us be sure that we make acts of confidence at one time, of devotion at another, and again of love of his never-ending goodness. Let us at one time be thanking him for his favors and at another time rejoicing in his glory, and again asking counsel in our doubts, and consoling ourselves always because we possess this Sovereign Good within us. We should be certain that no created power can take him from us, and that he will never depart from us unless we first voluntarily banish him from our hearts.

This was the little cell that St. Catherine of Siena built within her heart, to which she always retired, always engaged in loving conversations with God. In this way she defended herself against the persecution of her parents, who had forbidden her to retire anymore to her chamber to pray. And in this little cell she always remained in the presence of God.

The True Spouse of Jesus Christ

Depend on the Intercession of the Martyrs

We should recommend ourselves every day with great confidence to the intercession of the holy martyrs, whose prayers are most effective with God. When we suffer some grievous pain or when we desire a special favor, let us make a novena or triduum in honor of the holy martyrs, and we will easily obtain the grace. Let us not fail to honor them, says St. Ambrose, for they are our princes in the faith and our powerful intercessors.

If the Lord promises a reward to him who gives a drink of water to a poor man (Matthew 25:34-35), what will he not do for those who sacrificed their lives in the midst of torments! Let us here observe that the martyrs, before receiving the mortal blow, without doubt prepared themselves many times for the many tortures and for death, so that when they closed their earthly career, they died with the crown not only of one martyrdom but of all those martyrdoms they had already accepted and offered sincerely to God. Therefore, we can only imagine with what abundance of merits they entered heaven and how valuable is their mediation with God.

Voice of the Martyrs

Sources and Acknowledgments

All texts in this book are adapted from volumes previously published as part of *The Complete Aesthetical Works of St. Alphonsus de Liguori*, as listed below:

De Liguori, Alphonsus, and Eugene Grimm, ed. *Preparation for Death*. Brooklyn: Redemptorist Fathers: 1926. (Volume I)

De Liguori, Alphonsus, and Eugene Grimm, ed. *The Way of Salvation and of Perfection*. Brooklyn: Redemptorist Fathers: 1926. (Volume II)

De Liguori, Alphonsus, and Eugene Grimm, ed. *The Great Means of Salvation and of Perfection*. Brooklyn: Redemptorist Fathers: 1927. (Volume III)

De Liguori, Alphonsus, and Eugene Grimm, ed. *The Incarnation, Birth and Infancy of Jesus Christ*. Brooklyn: Redemptorist Fathers: 1927. (Volume IV)

De Liguori, Alphonsus, and Eugene Grimm, ed. *The Passion and the Death of Jesus Christ*. New York: Benziger Brothers, 1886. (Volume V)

De Liguori, Alphonsus, and Eugene Grimm, ed. *The Holy Eucharist*. Brooklyn: Redemptorist Fathers, 1934. (Volume VI)

De Liguori, Alphonsus, and Eugene Grimm, ed.
The Glories of Mary. Brooklyn: Redemptorist Fathers,
1931. (Volume VII and VIII in one).

De Liguori, Alphonsus, and Eugene Grimm, ed.
Victories of the Martyrs. Brooklyn: Redemptorist Fathers:
1954. (Volume IX)

De Liguori, Alphonsus, and Eugene Grimm, ed.
The True Spouse of Jesus Christ. Brooklyn: Redemptorist
Fathers: 1929. (Volume X and XI)

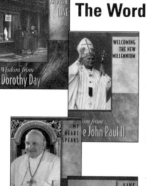

Other titles from
The Word Among Us Press Wisdom Series

A Radical Love:
Wisdom from Dorothy Day

Welcoming the New Millennium:
Wisdom from Pope John Paul II

My Heart Speaks:
Wisdom from Pope John XXIII

Live Jesus! Wisdom from Saints Francis
de Sales and Jane de Chantal

Love Songs:
Wisdom from St. Bernard
of Clairvaux

Walking with the Father:
Wisdom from Brother Lawrence

Touching the Risen Christ:
Wisdom from The Fathers

Hold Fast to God:
Wisdom from The Early Church

Even Unto Death:
Wisdom from Modern Martyrs

These popular books include short biographies of the authors and selections from their writings grouped around themes such as prayer, forgiveness, and mercy.